Charles Gilmer has been laboring in the vineyard of our Lord for a long time. He has learned significant lessons along the way. I count him as a friend and commend him to you.

—Steve Douglass
President
Campus Crusade for Christ International

Every now and then, God uses a plumb line to point to something to which He wants to direct our attention. In communities of African descent that plumb line points to our need for Him. God has wonderfully orchestrated Charles' life in such a way that he is an encouraging reminder of what all of us should be about. His story compellingly illustrates what it takes to minister to these communities in effective ways in order to see as many people as possible experience the hope and love of Jesus Christ.

—Dr. Crawford W. Loritts, Jr.
Author and Radio Host
Sr. Pastor, Fellowship Bible Church
Roswell, GA

People are different. That's really not a new realization. But when it comes to how we influence different groups of people, we sometimes forget that. What Charles and Rebecca Gilmer are doing through The Impact Movement is a marked move of God's Spirit in the lives of those of African descent. Let's join them in whatever way we can to see change at the deepest level: that of the heart.

—Dr. Joel C. Hunter
Senior Pastor

There is a cry that is ringing from weary hearts. Many are seeking a cure for the emptiness that ails them and Charles Gilmer, along with The Impact Movement, is sending out a call for anyone with a heart willing to heed. This man and this ministry have been an enormous blessing in my life for well over a decade. A peek inside these pages will unveil a vision, passion, integrity, and mission that will endear you to this unbelievable ministry. Prepare to be blessed.

—Priscilla Shirer
Author and Speaker

I've known Charles and his wife, Rebecca, for a long time. I've worked alongside them, and we have prayed for each other. I've seen them face up to challenges, weather storms, and celebrate victories. They are people with a passion for Christ and for reaching others. Their vision for and commitment to communities of African descent inspires hope for the future. The Impact Movement is uniquely positioned to raise up a generation of leaders dependent on Jesus Christ to transform lives. And that makes all the difference.

—Andrea Buczynski
Vice President
Global Leadership Development
Campus Crusade for Christ International

I don't know of any other organization that targets young people of African descent with the same significance as The Impact Movement. The great thing about The Impact Movement is that it's not just talk. I've seen young people enter their ministry in all kinds of conditions and leave inspired, knowing that all things are possible with God. I know. I was one of them.

—Pastor Keith Battle
Lead Pastor, Zion Church

There are few with whom I feel a greater connection in the work of our Lord than I do with Charles Gilmer. The work that the Lord has called him to is great and significant. And it is God's business. To minister to people in the idioms of culture while introducing them to the God who created it—and them—is an amazing thing. Who would not want to be a part? I invite you to not miss the invitation.

—DR. DELA ADADEVOH
INTERNATIONAL VICE PRESIDENT
CAMPUS CRUSADE FOR CHRIST

A Cry of Hope, a Call to Action confirms God's glorious call to The Impact Movement to mobilize an army of "modern-day Josephs" whose slave ancestors four centuries ago were providentially pulled from Africa—which has been ravished by disease, AIDS, drought, floods, famine, collapsing economies, and civil wars—to now help save their brothers and sisters in the motherland and throughout the diaspora from a coming "seven-year famine" of devastation and desolation (tribulation). You want to read how God uniquely destined Impact to ignite a last-days' global evangelical movement that will surely usher many souls into Christ's eternal kingdom! It is destiny unfolding!

—RACHELLE HOOD
FOUNDER, THE EPHRAIM PROJECT
IMPACT BOARD MEMBER
FORMER CHIEF DIVERSITY OFFICER, DENNY'S
CORPORATION

Charles Gilmer is an African American who knows what it is like to live in an evangelical world dominated by White culture. His personal story is one of accomplishment and pride in his Black heritage. It is also the story of a Black Christian deeply committed to reaching other African Americans for Christ. His experience and convictions have given birth to The Impact Movement—a vibrant ministry to African American college students. This is a timely book and one much needed in our day. Read it and you will see the world in living color.

—Dr. Frank A. James
Provost
Gordon-Conwell Theological Seminary

Charles and Rebecca Gilmer have been on the front lines of "guerilla evangelism" for years. Charles' book unveils this unique and historic ministry in an engaging way. This is a story that will encourage, inspire, and challenge you to live fully for Jesus.

—Nannette Turner, PhD, MPH
Assistant Professor
Mercer University School of Medicine

I love social change. But I know that it's not enough. Through Rev. Gilmer's story we rediscover that it is not the surface of a leader that can bring transformation. It is the power of the gospel lived out through His people. Rev. Gilmer points us to what it will take to see this kind of transformation happen on a broad scale in our community.

—O'Hara C. Black
Senior Pastor
Mount Pleasant Missionary Baptist Church

A CRY OF
HOPE
A CALL TO
ACTION

CHARLES GILMER

CREATION
HOUSE
A STRANG COMPANY

A CRY OF HOPE, A CALL TO ACTION by Charles Gilmer
Published by Creation House
A Strang Company
600 Rinehart Road
Lake Mary, Florida 32746
www.strangbookgroup.com

Unless otherwise noted, all Scripture quotations are from the Holy Bible, New International Version of the Bible. Copyright © 1973, 1978, 1984, International Bible Society. Used by permission.

Photo credits: photo top of page 105 by Jamaica Gilmer; front and back cover, bottom of page 106, and photos on pages 107–108 by Allen Stanley.

Design Director: Bill Johnson
Cover design by Karen Gonsalves
Interior design by Annette Simpson

Library of Congress Control Number: 2008939242

International Standard Book Number: 978-1-59979-605-5

First Edition

09 10 11 12 13 — 9 8 7 6 5 4 3 2 1

Printed in the United States of America

CONTENTS

www.CharlesGilmer.com

ACKNOWLEDGMENTS

FIRST AND FOREMOST, I must thank my wife and partner in ministry, Rebecca. The editing process caused you to be less visible on these pages than I originally intended. The reality is that there is not a single story in which you are not present, even when I did not yet know you. You are the one I was always looking for, the one whose absence I felt as loneliness, the one I prayed for and whom God prepared and protected for me. It remains true that the single most obvious evidence of God's intent to use me is His giving you to me to be my *ezer*. You have been my biggest fan, my most honest critic, and the love of my life. You have impacted my life in just about every way possible, and I am always challenged to stay ahead of your strength as a leader. May God continue to grant you grace to extend grace, mercy, and love to this most imperfect servant, who stumbles and fumbles his way through trying to show you that he loves you. Because I do. Six children later, you are still as beautiful as the day I met you.

To my children, Micah, Jared, Daniel, Karis, Caleb, and Joy: I love you more than you can fathom. Being your father is my greatest accomplishment.

To the women who married my sons, Jamaica, Brittany, and Chanel: you are each just what I prayed for. I am delighted to call each of you my daughter.

Also, thanks to:

Dennis Talbert, you have never been part of the staff of The Impact Movement, but you are very much a part of our story.

You may have been the earliest to recommend that I write (except for my Rebecca and Tom Fritz).

My friend Dr. Rodney Orr, who acknowledged my life's work and encouraged me to write now, not later.

Jeff Pagliolonga and Dan and Shelia Broughton, who allowed me to use their properties to get away, focus, and write.

Chip Scivique and Dan Hardaway, who have been partners in ministry with Campus Crusade for Christ, always pressing the envelope to see more students reached.

To The Impact Movement executive team, past (Jim and Shanera Williamson, Jacqueline Bland, Anthony and Angela Johnson, Kevin and Patricia Werst, Lisa Hudson, Shelia Maxwell Adams, Sam and Eva Johnson, Terry and Nina Alexander, and the legendary Bobby Herron) and present (Chris and Jo Restuccia, Dirke and Lorna Johnson, Rose Thompson, Allen Stanley, Greg Hersey, Scott and Lori Crocker, Jermayne and Meredith Chapman, and Melody Gardner): it has been and is an honor to serve with you.

To The Impact Movement board (Keith Battle, Adrian Barfield, Rachelle Hood, David Lawson, Marcus Littles, Dionne Lomax, Esq., Dr. Nannette Turner, and Dr. Earl Wilson): it's good to know that you all "got my back."

Our team at Howard—Linda Youngblood, Marcella Charles, and James White; later, Cynthia Turner White, David and Edwina Hamlin Perkins, Belinda Watkins, Rod and Sheri Austin Hairston, Janice Johnson, Melvita Chisolm, and for a minute, Derrick Lovick.

Keijo Hunter, for all your work to get this book in print. You were the MVP of this process, working on the stories and managing the overall process. You are like gold!

Dr. Frank James, Tim Turner, and Judy Nelson, who were honest enough to tell me when the manuscript wasn't quite there yet. Your editorial contributions were invaluable. And to Erik Segalini, who helped us edit the stories that helped to reveal the power of the movement described herein.

Dirke Johnson, for being a collaborator on my thinking about reconciliation and contextualization.

Bekele Shanko, for your faith, challenge, and inspiration.

Dr. Dela Adadevoh, for your encouragement, intellect, and pan-African vision.

Naton Kamanga, for your boldness and admiration.

James White, my brother in the struggle. We have walked many miles, yet there are many yet to come.

Steve Sellers, my friend, mentor, and sponsor. Your willingness to risk in order to achieve an eternal reward will ever challenge me. I am glad that we will always be on the same team.

John Rogers, my fellow member of the six-kid club. You are the best, and I will always be grateful for the ways you make it possible to "get it done."

Mark Gauthier, my turf rescuer and fellow pilgrim. I only wish I had had the chance to serve under you. It would have been a privilege.

Mike Tilley, my former boss and later coconspirator. You were a great guardian of what we were doing at Howard. I miss talking politics and economics with you.

Andrea Buczynski. What can we say? This is the first in our published memoirs. We heard you.

Holly Sheldon. You came out of nowhere (OK, China) to encourage us at a key season. "Thank you" is not enough.

Steve Douglass. Your grace, innovativeness, humility, and will to get out of the way have been an amazing thing to watch and benefit from. I have known several great men. You are one of them.

Jim Keller. It's been a while, but I will never forget your belief in me.

John Mackin. God had you in the right place at the right time for me. It could have been the other way.

Micah Gilmer, my collaborator, editor, researcher, would-be literary agent, and firstborn son. Thank you for prodding me to get started on this. Your support and encouragement mean more than you know.

Thomas Fritz. What can I possibly say? We have walked this path for nearly thirty years. Model, teacher, trainer. Mentor, leader, developer. Confidante, counselor, coconspirator. Prayer warrior, friend, Keeper of the Dream...

Anna Gilmer. Mom, thank you for believing in me. Your sacrifices are noted, and you will be rewarded.

The Reverend Paul Gilmer, my father. I know you are watching as a part of that "cloud of witnesses" (Heb. 12:1). Thank you for the gift of being able to watch you live and lead. Your encouragement to remain that watchman "on the wall" still rings in my ears. Thank you for those final words.

Others come to mind, like all the Impact staff; our donors; the First Baptist Church of Vandalia; the late Reverend Earl Nobles; the late J. T. Walker; my old Ethnic Student Ministries regional directors, Shane Dieke, Jim Topmiller, Michael and Ann Christopher, Jim and Jane Corman, Bob and Shirley Shirock, Nick Foley, Clarence Otis and Jacqui Bradley, and Christopher and Jackie Lynch.

1
CRISIS AT THE CAPSTONE

W HAT ARE WE going to do with all this chicken? For a young, married missionary with two small children, an abundance of food would have otherwise been considered a blessing, were it not actually a feast born from the failure of one of our initial outreaches at Howard University.

I reflected on all that we had done to prepare for this, our first freshmen cookout as Campus Crusade for Christ at Howard University. I had rented a fifteen-passenger van to shuttle Howard University students from campus to the park we had scouted out for this Labor Day event. As I drove through northwest Washington, DC, my primary concern was that the pavilion we selected would no longer be available to us since reservations were not allowed on such a busy day.

The rest of the team was still busy with food preparation. Marcella and Linda, two of our staff, had spent the previous evening frying enough chicken to feed the anticipated crowd of fifty. My wife, Rebecca, pitched in, preparing salads while juggling the needs of our two preschool boys. My mind had percolated with excitement about the games and other activities we had planned to connect with these new students, all of whom had filled out a spiritual interest questionnaire, indicating that they wanted to know more about Christ or participate in a small group Bible study.

While driving up to the Fourth Street gate, I was pleased to see one of our handful of returning students. During the

previous year, 1984, our first on Howard's campus, we organized one men's and two women's small group Bible studies.
And we ended the year with a coed fellowship meeting much
like the one we planned for the following week to kick off this
school and ministry year.

As we sat and waited for the first twelve to arrive so that
I could commence the shuttling process, I wondered how we
would notify the others that I was coming back to pick them
up. Unfortunately, I had a lot of time to think about that and
any number of other things. The five minutes turned to twenty,
then sixty, when the cold reality set in that those forty-nine
other confirmed attendees were not going to show up. So the
solitary student who had arrived and our four-person staff
adjourned to our row house (a "semi-detached home," as our
realtor was fond of saying) on North Capitol Street and held a
fried chicken feast.

As we froze all that leftover chicken and divvied up the salads
and drinks that evening, I pondered what it would take to see
the movement of young people emerge that I was called to serve
and committed to reaching. If we couldn't coax college students
to attend a free cookout, how in the world were we going to
be able to convince them to participate in the overwhelmingly
White ministry of Campus Crusade for Christ? There was only
so much leftover fried chicken that I was willing to eat!

As hundreds of the more than two thousand attendees of
Impact 2006 stream to the front of the ballroom to sign The
Impact Movement Commitment, I am struck by the readiness
of the students and alumni that are doing so. The ballroom
of the Atlanta Omni Hotel quiets as I pray, somber reflection
slowly giving way to the anticipation and ultimate celebration
of a New Year as I close in prayer at midnight. The room erupts

in praise and thanksgiving to God as we welcome 2007, the sounds quickly giving way to a hip-hop beat as gospel hip-hop artist Flame leaps to the stage. They have signed a commitment to invest themselves in Christ's Great Commission from the perspective of their newly clarified identity as Christians of African descent. Some do not trace their roots to Africa, yet they still sign due to their commitment to seeing such a movement take place.

The conferees, mostly college students, are thankful for how God has used them to expose more than 2,500 people to the gospel in Atlanta the day before, and for the 300 who indicated that they placed their faith in Christ for salvation. Sobriety over the suffering that hovers over our community mingles with anticipation of how God will work out the specifics of the visions and dreams He has placed in their hearts over the last several days. Yet, in that moment their seriousness is overwhelmed by the sheer joy of their usefulness to God; the comfort and encouragement of having spent five days with two thousand people who look like them, talk like them, sing like them, are moved by the same things as that which moves them, and are concerned about the same things that concern them. Things like the challenge of living a godly lifestyle as a single black professional. The frustration over the subtle racism they experience every day. Will they ever find a Christian mate? The questions coursing through their minds about the reliability of the Bible, the need to integrate their Christian faith with their academic development, and the relevance and applicability of the gospel to their twenty-first century existence.

They've made new friends, learned new principles, and discovered new opportunities for service. They want to tell their friends what they have just experienced. Some want to start an Impact chapter on their campus, while others want to take their existing chapter to new levels. Some have been called to the mission field. Others know they are to pastor, teach, or start a business or new ministry. It's a little scary, but they know they can trust Him to bring it to pass.

This is quite a different picture than that Labor Day in 1984. God is clearly moving in dramatic, far-reaching ways. But, I know that we are only getting started. Our time at Howard demonstrated itself to be a fertile proving ground for the principles that are yielding the fruit we now call The Impact Movement. The identification of those principles and their application was a long and arduous process. Not only were we wrestling with the challenge of connecting with a dynamic, unique leadership culture in the Black college student and the burgeoning Black professional class, but we also were contending with the dynamics of doing so as part of the largest predominantly White para-church organization in the U.S.

This story is a very personal one for me. It is the account of the revelation and clarification of my calling. It is also one that touches the experience of millions of African Americans, perhaps that of even more who trace their roots back to Africa from various parts of the African diaspora. This story connects to Africa itself in some ways that are clear and in some ways that await discovery. In order to understand it, I want to walk you, the reader, through some formative influences in my life. I hope to help you understand where we are going with this movement we call Impact, but this story is most clearly understood in light of where we have been.

2
CONNECTING WITH THE CULTURE

H OWARD UNIVERSITY, A sprawling urban campus, is
located just north of Washington, DC's, central business district. Howard has a very collegial central yard,
a large number of dormitory residents, and an extremely active
social life. It draws eleven thousand students from across the
U.S., Africa, and the Caribbean

African Americans are part of the African diaspora, the
dispersion of people of African descent around the world. The
slave trade, which took a triangular path from Africa; to Brazil,
the Caribbean Islands, and the U.S.; and back to Europe was
a major contributor to this dispersion, creating massive Black
populations in each of these areas. But the trans-Saharan slave
trade actually predated that historical phenomenon, sending
Africans into the near Asian regions. Some suggest that the
South Pacific islanders of Fiji, Samoa, New Zealand, and the
aborigines of Australia ought to be considered an even more
ancient part of that dispersion.

We had eight Campus Crusade for Christ staff assigned to
work with students at Howard at our peak from 1987–1992, but
we never had more than four active on campus at the same time.
Campus Crusade for Christ is a faith-ministry, requiring each
of its missionary staff to develop the funds that person needs to
cover their salary and personal ministry expenses. The task was
more of a challenge for many of us Black Campus Crusade staff
to accomplish than our White counterparts, so we never were

all on campus at the same time because of the need to focus on securing funding.

The dean of the chapel at Howard University, Dr. Evans Crawford, welcomed us to the campus. He recognized para-church workers as part of his chaplaincy program, giving us a formal identity on campus. He would sponsor our room requests and other administrative papers. Some chaplains at historically Black campuses were more restrictive in granting groups like ours access to students. Dean Crawford told stories illustrating his appreciation of the fact that we were connecting with students, making ourselves available to provide spiritual counsel long before many of them would ordinarily seek out the dean. As he said, "By the time they come to me, it is by and large too late. Most of the damage has already been done." Dean Crawford created a community at Howard where we, as well as other campus ministries, could operate with the blessing and facilitation of the chapel office.

I spent the first several weeks of my time there meeting the other campus ministers, both denominational and para-church. I also sought to connect with as many African-American pastors from the communities immediately surrounding Howard as I could. I spent a lot of time apologizing for a variety of offenses on the part of Campus Crusade for Christ. Some of these incidents were simple misunderstandings; others were evidences of blatant insensitivity. As I shared our story and our experience within Campus Crusade, there was acceptance and support, though that support was occasionally of a grudging nature. Washington, D.C., is the nation's capital, after all, and the Black community there was chafing under their perceived marginalization by President Ronald Reagan's administration. Rebecca and I were clear about our calling to serve as a part of Campus Crusade for Christ, but that identity was often greeted with skepticism in the Black community.

Our first outreach in the fall semester of 1984 was in October. We set up a survey table in the Blackburn Student Center, where virtually all freshmen campus residents were required to eat their meals. Students responded well to that survey. Over half of those who filled it out said that they wanted to talk more about what it meant to have a relationship with Christ. Even more indicated a willingness to participate in a Bible study. (That rate of response continued throughout our time at Howard.) The survey led to Bible studies in Drew Hall and the Harriet Tubman Quadrangle (the Quad), as well as the men's and women's freshman dorms.

That spring, we had our first fellowship meeting in a unique meeting area in the Human Ecology building at Howard called The Living Room. The summer of 1985 we brainstormed what to call the weekly coed meeting, and Rebecca suggested that we call it Living Color. This was five years before Kenan Ivory Wayans launched the television show *In Living Color,* which ran from 1990–1994. (Marlon Wayans was a student at Howard from 1990 to 1992.) It was also three years before the debut album of the rock band Living Colour. My wife has often been one step ahead of the times.

When the freshmen showed up on campus in August, we undertook a survey effort during freshman week. We had our first Living Color meeting, this time in the Forum in the student center. I introduced the meeting by saying, "Welcome to Living Color. Some people think the Christian life is out of date and second rate, like a black-and-white TV. We are here to declare that the Christian life is vibrant and exciting, the best life anyone can have."

That year (1985) we planned the big Labor Day picnic mentioned earlier. We figured that since students at Howard were from all over the country and the school observed every federal holiday, they needed a good Labor Day option.

Students were responding well to our surveys and our personal evangelistic follow-up, but there were a few things we were learning. One was that you could not call students to set up appointments as a survey follow-up and expect that effort to be fruitful.

Campus Crusade for Christ basic campus training stipulated that staff utilize Sunday nights to set up appointments for the week. Linda Youngblood, who graduated from UC Berkeley and had been on CCC staff at Cornell prior to her time at Howard, came to one of our staff meetings incredibly frustrated. She shared how she had diligently made her calls on Sunday evening and had filled her week with appointments. But, one of those days, all six students set to meet her in the Blackburn Center had failed to show up. I explained to Linda what Thomas Fritz, my original trainer and the pioneer of campus ministry among Black students within Campus Crusade for Christ, had taught me during my time in Atlanta. For one thing, at that time for the most part Black college dorms had hall payphones only, so the calling process was tedious and time consuming. Someone would answer the phone, and once you asked for the person you were trying to reach, you never knew whether the message would be delivered, if the person would even choose to take the call, or if he or she might get distracted on the way down the hall to the phone. Secondly, when students would set this type of appointment, they didn't view commitment to attendance as a character issue. They valued relationships and flexibility to such a degree that any number of things could preempt such a commitment.

The better method was to stop by students' rooms at times that you expected them to be there. That was a challenge due to the security that was in place at this inner-city campus, but once the dorm staff got to know us, we were allowed relatively free access.

Despite some of these frustrations, it was exciting to tackle the challenge of connecting with Howard students day after day. It was such a hotbed of Black cultural, ideological, and intellectual discourse. We were waging a war for the souls of the next generation of leaders.

Once James White arrived as a part of our team, he and I began a running conversation about how we could best communicate with students in our public speaking. We observed the distinctive presentation style of Louis Farrakhan and others. Students running for student association offices at Howard would imitate their cadence and intensity when they spoke. Other students adopted the style of the Black preacher. We concluded that if we wanted to operate in the cultural idioms of the students, we could not just "give a talk" in the manner that our Campus Crusade for Christ exposure and training had taught us. We began to communicate with more force and style. Students responded. The ministry grew.

One aid to this was the attitude of my CCC leaders. Mike Tilley, my direct supervisor, was incredibly teachable and respectful of the unique dynamic of our work at Howard. He would visit us once a year, and, unlike his visits to other campuses, he would forgo his customary address to the students. He approached his visits as learning opportunities. He was particularly tickled when we took him to a debate that another Christian organization sponsored between one of Louis Farrakhan's chief lieutenants and Tom Skinner, the African-American former gang leader who was a well-known Christian evangelist. Eventually, as our ministry at Howard grew and became more established, we did ask Mike to use his gifts as a Bible teacher to minister to the students.

My regional director, Jim Keller, understood our distinct challenge as well. When we planned his visit, he asked if he could speak on the topic of racism. Our team had to talk about it a bit, but we decided that if this White guy was brave enough to tackle that topic at Howard University, then who were we to stand in the way? I did ask him, however, if he and I could review his message together before he got in front of the students. He intended to describe his own pilgrimage in matters of race, and I told him I thought that could be good. He was going to include a personal anecdote in which he confessed using the word *nigger* at a track meet and getting his face slapped by an African American runner. I told him he could tell the story but not to utter the word. The confession is good, I told him, and we will be forgiving of that, but there is something inflammatory any time a White person lets that word pass their lips. He appreciated the feedback, gave a great message that night, and at Howard student attitudes toward Campus Crusade continued to be positive.

As he observed our work at Howard, Jim was very affirming of our efforts. We had around one hundred students involved at that point, a very respectably sized ministry for Campus Crusade at that time. He began to talk with me about my career in the organization in light of Campus Crusade's commitment to placing African-American leadership at all levels of the organization. He explained to me that he believed I had the potential to be an area director but that in order to be perceived as qualified for that role, I would need to lead a ministry on a predominantly White campus. I could follow his logic: if I were to be a Campus Crusade area director, I would be leading ministry in an area that encompassed a majority of White students. Therefore it seemed reasonable that I should demonstrate an ability to lead in a White ministry context. However, that was not at all that to which God had called me. My calling is clearly to the African-American community. The conversation with Jim was a poignant reminder of a decision I faced several years earlier.

Connecting with the Culture

By the time I graduated from high school in Dunbar, West Virginia, I had achieved a great deal. My senior year almost reads like something from a storybook. I lettered in three sports, was elected president of the student council, and was being recruited by the top colleges in the nation not as an athlete but as a student.

Graduation was fun. I spoke as the salutatorian, and I was recognized as a National Achievement Scholar and honorary National Merit Scholar. I was named a Presidential Scholar, one of only 121 in the nation. I attended the National Youth Science Camp and received the presidential scholarship to Cornell University in Ithaca, New York. I chose Cornell in part because Lloyd Slaughter, a Christian executive at Union Carbide Corporation, had seen a newspaper article about my academic and other achievements and recruited me to attend his alma mater. I liked the idea of getting out of West Virginia. I wanted to learn more about the rest of the world. Cornell paid my expenses to visit the campus, one of the most beautiful that I have seen. Several of the schools I considered were in big cities, and I didn't know if I was ready for that.

While I applied to the engineering school due to my love of math and science, I wasn't sure what I was going to do with my life. The thought of having to choose a career was becoming a source of anxiety for me, even before my high school graduation. I was equally capable in a variety of academic subjects and had a broad range of interests. I just liked learning and achieving. I began to pray about it and to think constantly about which path I would choose.

The principal of my high school went out of his way to set up a time to talk to me, advising me to become a medical doctor. The pressure of the decision began to give me a constant headache. I never had headaches before, nor do I today.

One night that spring I sat down to write my girlfriend, who lived in Philadelphia. I had met her at a Minority Introduction to Engineering (MITE) summer program, and we had been corresponding since then. As I began to write, the idea of going into ministry came into my mind. I was startled by the sudden cessation of my headache. It was just gone. The significance of the dramatic change was clear to me. I understood that this was my call from God to serve Him.

I reported this experience in my letter and got up from the table to tell my dad what had just happened. My dad was a prominent pastor in W. Virginia and was often sought out by other ministers for his counsel. His advice upon hearing my story was simple and sound: "Take your time. If that is what God wants you to do, that is what you will do. Get a good liberal arts education. But don't be in a hurry to make this public."

I particularly appreciated the last words he gave me. He encouraged me to take it slow in announcing my call because he had seen many a young man make a public pronouncement, only to fall into sin or otherwise fail to live up to the promise such an acknowledgement implies. Growing up the son of a Baptist preacher, I, too, had seen it happen many times.

From that point on, I began quietly to make decisions in light of this calling. I began to shadow my father a bit as he fulfilled his pastoral responsibilities. But, pastoring was not the picture God had planted in my mind. I sensed that his path was not mine. Neither was being a foreign missionary. I had some brief exposure to missionaries, but mission work in another country did not seem to be what God was directing me to do.

I had read lots of Black history, and my mind and heart were suffused with stories from the Civil Rights Movement. My exposure was more than book learning. My mother had grown up in the First Baptist Church of Charleston, West Virginia, where Mordecai Johnson, the president of West Virginia State

University, served as pastor. My aunt and uncle were leaders in that church, so I was there periodically. During my teen years, the pastor of First Baptist was a son of Ebenezer Baptist Church in Atlanta, the home church of Rev. Dr. Martin Luther King, Jr. The Morehouse Glee Club would perform there on a regular basis. My parents served on the board of the local chapter of the NAACP, so I was exposed to stories of our people's struggle not just through my reading but through hearing noted preachers in the pulpits of our small city and via conversations at the dinner table when we would host visiting church leaders.

The best way I could describe my vision was that it was an echo or an evolution of the ministry of Dr. King, building on what he had done but with more of an emphasis on calling people to spiritual commitment. The Civil Rights Movement had drawn so much of its energy from Christian faith and had captured the imagination and aspirations of the emerging young leaders of the Black community. Yet, as I was coming of age, the church was losing so many young people. Our emerging Black middle class seemed bent on a life of self-indulgence and materialism. Doors of opportunity were swinging open, and we were eager to make our mark on and enjoy the fruits of broader American society. We wrestled, on the one hand, with the incessant burden of having to perform in order to prove that you belonged in the mainstream marketplace, and on the other hand living in both fear and attraction to the dangerous underbelly of Black culture. There had to be a way to call the emerging generation of African Americans to make the most of that for which so many had marched, prayed, endured hardship and beatings, and for which Dr. King and others had died. My calling was to find that way and sound that cry.

3

EXPLORATIONS OF RECONCILIATION

Back at Howard University, as a part of Campus Crusade for Christ we were expected to participate in the variety of gatherings that CCC created to bring students together from different campuses for training, motivation, and fellowship. We attended all the major conferences of Campus Crusade for Christ. That was a big deal for us and the students in that at Howard most people did not realize that Campus Crusade for Christ was anything other than a predominantly Black organization. All they saw of Campus Crusade for Christ was our team, which remained all Black for the entire ten years we had staff at Howard. A decisive correction of that perception occurred any time we attended a Campus Crusade event away from Howard University.

The first such event we attended was a fall retreat. The Howard students were excited about getting out of the city, seeing the fall foliage, and learning more about God. We staff knew that we would be there with Campus Crusade students from the University of Maryland, Towson State, West Virginia University, and other universities. We decided not to make a big deal of the interracial nature of the event. The subject failed to surface during our first fall retreat recruiting effort in 1985—until seven or so students who had preregistered to attend were in the van with me on the way to the retreat.

Marcella Charles, a veteran CCC staff member and part of our team, pointed out to me that we ought to warn them of the reality that our students were likely to be in the minority at the retreat, so I pulled the van over and said, "You do know, don't you, that Campus Crusade for Christ is not a predominantly Black organization?" The dumbfounded looks on the faces of the students let me know that the question had not crossed their minds.

One student asked, "How many people will be there?" I replied, "About two hundred."

"How many will be Black?" they continued to process.

I stated in a matter-of-fact manner, "I am not sure, but we may be it."

"Oh," was the somewhat stunned reply.

Now, most of those students had had plenty of exposure to White people. The majority of the students at Howard had attended predominantly White high schools, but, like me, their Christian experience prior to college had been in an African-American cultural setting. Those who had just become believers at Howard had not had any Christian activity in a White setting.

While some may question the wisdom of the timing of my disclosure that the retreat was not an all-Black event, the Howard students were real troopers about it all. They wanted to grow in their relationship with Jesus, and this was a great opportunity and setting to do just that. They did, however, find it a bit hard to relate to the music. Acoustic guitar is not the instrument of choice in Black Christian circles. For their part, the White students, most of whom were very young or immature in their faith, were a mixed bag of racial attitudes and experiences. A low-level awkwardness would periodically heighten due to an insensitive comment or question. But, on the whole, it was a rich and meaningful experience for the Howard students who attended.

Back on campus after the retreat, the Howard students became great walking advertisements for the event. As years went by and the ministry grew, our fall retreat attendance increased accordingly. I looked forward to the day when our numbers would be large enough to change the cultural flavor of the conference, and our students would relate not as a minority presence but as a peer presence.

We also sought to get students to attend the Campus Crusade Christmas conference, held between Christmas and New Year's Day. While several were held regionally around the country, the one that we were to attend was in Philadelphia. Rebecca and I are graduates of the University of Pennsylvania. We met and spent our first year of marriage in "The City of Brotherly Love," so returning to Philly sounded fun to me. Unfortunately, the typical Campus Crusade Christmas conferences were mostly a wasted effort in terms of our work at Howard.

Due to the nationwide scope of enrollment at Howard University, getting people to return from their homes in the middle of the Christmas break for such an event was tough. In addition, there was the often-unspoken obstacle of choosing to spend four days with over one thousand White college students, singing acoustic guitar-led praise songs, and listening to speakers who, every now and then, would say something alienating or offensive. I think the most we ever saw attend was seven, and those seven were scattered over three different Christmas conferences—Philadelphia, Atlanta, and Chicago. Not the best scenario for generating momentum and camaraderie. Rebecca and I kept looking for conference venues that would connect with Howard students due to the distinct role a conference had played in our lives and ministry.

While I started my college career at Cornell University, I transferred to the University of Pennsylvania in Philadelphia for two reasons. I was still in the long-distance relationship with the girl I met at the MITE program at the University of Pittsburgh. She attended Temple University in Philadelphia, and I figured it was time to find out whether that relationship was "the one" or not. I also had my interest in urban Black culture fueled by my Black dormitory mates at Ujamaa Residential College at Cornell. Most of them were from New York City, and despite my small-city origins, their accounts gave me a greater sense of my ability to make my way in an urban setting.

When I transferred to the University of Pennsylvania, the relationship ended rather quickly, but my Black cultural and intellectual exposure continued. I chose to live in another Black studies living–learning program, the W.E.B. DuBois College House. I attended a Bible study that met at Dubois, and coincidentally, this one had ties to Campus Crusade for Christ. At the Bible study, I saw a coed I had seen at my first Black Student League meeting and subsequently was introduced to at a party. She was from New Orleans, and while quite attractive, she was a year ahead of me in school and according to my 19-year-old mind, not quite my type. She was light-skinned (I had a preference for brown-skinned girls), beautiful, and very self-confident. Still, Rebecca Guillory and I became friends as we both grew in our involvement with Campus Crusade for Christ.

For spring break, Campus Crusade for Christ (CCC) was taking a delegation to Daytona Beach, Florida, for an outreach conference called Operation Sunshine. A number of students from the Black Bible study decided to make the trip. We went there to engage the other spring break students in conversation about their spiritual state. Of course, this was the last thing on their minds, as they had made the trek south for some sun and some fun and were widely known for their raucous, rowdy, racy parties. Our purpose was to help them understand how they could know Jesus Christ in a personal way. We used a booklet,

The Four Spiritual Laws, to communicate the Bible's teachings on establishing a relationship with God in a simple way.

We saw many people indicate a decision to accept Christ, and one of the stars of the week was Rebecca. Her winsome personality and bold confidence made her an incredibly effective evangelist.

Our most significant experience occurred away from the beach during an afternoon at Bethune-Cookman College (now Bethune-Cookman University), a small historically Black school in Daytona Beach. There weren't many Black students on the beach, and many of us wanted to reach people who looked like us, so an afternoon of outreach at Bethune-Cookman was organized. We encountered a great deal of openness on the part of the students there. I had conversations with several Christians who wanted to know who we were and why we were there. Their universal response was, "We could use a group like this on our campus."

Rebecca had several people pray with her to ask Christ into their lives. As I got in the van that was to take us back to the beach, I asked a Campus Crusade staff member why there was no ongoing ministry on that campus. His answer was simple— because there was no staff member to go. They had discovered having Black staff workers was often a key to effective ministry to Black campus audiences, but Campus Crusade did not have enough staff to send someone to every school, and a small campus like Bethune-Cookman did not make the cut. He went on to explain the even more acute shortage of Black people on the staff of CCC.

I sat there listening to his words, but it was as if God were speaking to me. I knew at that moment that God wanted me to help change that reality. This was the vehicle through which I could take the next step in the calling I had received as I left high school. I was to help provide a ministry of Christian outreach and ongoing spiritual growth to Black college students, who I had discovered were underserved in this respect, as they were in so many other ways.

Five minutes later, Rebecca got on the bus and asked the same question of the same staff member. God was giving us a common burden and a shared vision of what He wanted to do with us, even at that early stage in our relationship.

Rebecca and I were just friends when we went to Daytona, increasingly special friends. We chose to attend the same short-term mission project that summer in Wildwood, New Jersey. It was a rich time of growth for both of us. Wildwood was a racist place, and Rebecca ended up working as a waitress at a boardwalk coffee shop after being turned away from several breakfast restaurants because she was Black. I got a job at a lumberyard, working my way up from yard hand to delivery driver. I got called a *nigger* and was spat on one day while walking from the mission project house to the church where we had our evening training time. Through all of these things we forged some relationships at Wildwood that have lasted to this day and grew deeper and stronger in our faith.

My and Rebecca's relationship continued to blossom through that shared experience. The Bible teaching on the project prodded us to ask deep questions of ourselves. The living environment—guys with guys, girls with girls—was in incredibly close quarters, which forced unexpected crises of personal growth. It was difficult to avoid working through conflict and seeing your own selfishness. The training and experience in ministry gave all of us a taste of what it is like to have God use you. As we went through and processed this experience together, we found our hearts drawn closer and closer together. Rebecca was and is such a gifted leader; I found her every thought an inspiration. Her experience growing up in an urban, transition neighborhood in New Orleans was a rich complement to my more static, semi-rural West Virginia experience. I was smitten, and I didn't really know it.

After we left the project, it didn't take long for me to wake up and realize that I was "in deep." I became convinced that Rebecca was the one for which I had been asking God. On September 11, 1979, I asked Rebecca to marry me. We were wed in May 1980. With her as my partner, we have together trusted God to bring into existence the vision He planted in me at the end of high school and clarified that day at Bethune-Cookman. Rebecca has been my greatest ally, a most aggressive critical thinker, and one of the best spokespersons for the ministry I know. I have learned a great deal from her and would not be the leader I am today without her help, input, and partnership. Oh, and it doesn't hurt that she is the most beautiful woman I have ever seen! She is my very personal illustration that Matthew 6:33 is true.

At Howard, we found the students quite receptive to the idea of repeating our experience in Daytona Beach by participating in CCC's spring break outreach there. The trip was quite popular with Howard students. My and Rebecca's experience caused us to be credible recruiters. The fact that Howard students hail from across the nation was no obstacle since for spring break students would be coming and going from campus. Actually, Howard had a strong history of students going on spring break excursions. The ski club, which sponsored a spring break ski trip to Colorado, was one of the largest on campus. Others would go to the Bahamas for Junkanoo, a Christmas season carnival held on those islands. So, the idea of a place where Christian students could go for spring break and would benefit spiritually was culturally relevant.

Some students were concerned about the expenses of the trip.

Very few had the resources to pay for it out of their pockets. However, over the years, we saw students raise thousands of dollars to allow them to attend these events. We put in place a letter-writing strategy for them to raise the funds, which we adapted from one that Campus Crusade for Christ had made available to students when organizing KC83, a national gathering of eighteen thousand students. Over the years, we challenged students to trust that if they wrote just ten letters, God would provide for their needs. During the eight years we were at Howard, God provided every nickel needed for every student who wrote the ten letters we asked him or her to write.

Despite our successes, my aspirations that the strength of our ministry at Howard could influence the face, mind, and culture of Campus Crusade proved to be a vain hope. The first disappointments came at the spring break conference, Operation Sunshine, in Daytona Beach. While our students willingly and admirably engaged others in the cross-cultural evangelistic challenge on the beaches, the battle to fit in with Campus Crusade was a nagging problem. Some Black folk like the beach a lot, but many are less than enthusiastic. Not surprisingly, the notion of trying to get a tan is not of value to most of us. Yet, nearly every year, there was a slogan, theme song, or an emcee remark that made our students feel like the event programmers discounted their presence. This continued even as our numbers swelled to fifty or so staff and students making the seventeen-hour trek.

The fall retreat was perhaps the most disappointing, though. Our attendance at the event grew until one year we took more than sixty students with us. The entire retreat attendance was only two hundred or so, so we were a significant presence in the audience. We had begun the practice of having special briefings for the students to prepare them for the odd racial comment or the uncomfortable moment, encouraging them to reach out to their fellow students despite the racial distinctions that were quite visible at the event. For these Howard students, interacting with White students was not a necessity. Most if not all of them had abundant experience relating to White people. In another sense, we invested the time to make sure that our students would have biblical motivation and spiritual power to engage in these cross-cultural exchanges. For these Howard students, dealing with White students was not a necessity in their day-to-day lives. Having to do so in order to grow spiritually required a little extra effort.

I was disappointed by the responses of the White students. They were a bit standoffish, sometimes rude, and often competitive with our Howard students. We occasionally heard comments like, "I don't like that kind of music. Could you turn it off?" when walking into a cabin where a Howard student was playing contemporary gospel music. Other students requested our students to leave a cabin so that a group could stay together with their friends. Of course, the typical uninformed and slightly invasive questions about hair or other obvious areas of difference were common as well.

Once there were enough Black students not to be a novelty anymore, the culture of the retreat no longer defaulted to what the White students were most comfortable with, and they didn't like it. I concluded that the idea of reconciliation, or more accurately living out the unity of the faith, is best engaged once a person has some degree of spiritual foundation and not before. A fall retreat is an event designed to help students who are at the point of deciding to walk with Jesus make that commitment or for those who have started on that journey to bond with others who are in a position to help them walk that walk in their own context. So, a call to work through one's racial issues is a lot to ask of a person who is still deciding to stop having sex with her boyfriend or to cease his drinking binges on the weekend.

Conversely, it is also unwise to ask Black students who are at a similar point to make accommodations to the racial insensitivity displayed and unwitting offenses committed by those who are accustomed to enjoying what Peggy McIntosh described as "White privilege" in her 1988 essay.[1]

WHY WHITES AND BLACKS APPROACH RACIAL MATTERS DIFFERENTLY

I, like most Black people, have been keenly aware of my "Blackness" since I was a child. From multiple conversations with friends, I know that most White Americans do not have a sense of their "Whiteness." The sense of being something different is only discovered when thrust into a predominantly ethnic setting, where Black or other ethnic Americans feel free to be themselves. In those settings we reveal thoughts, attitudes, and behaviors that we have learned not to disclose as we operate in mainstream American culture.

One of my earliest memories was sitting on my mother's lap as a four year old watching the news as Walter Cronkite described footage of German Shepherds attacking peaceful protestors on the CBS Evening News. He referred repeatedly to "Negroes," prompting me to ask my mother, "What's a Negro?" Her answer, a simple, "We are," was stunning to me. My father and my uncle were firemen, and my neighbor (who was also Black) was a policeman, so I thought of people in uniform as the good guys. This revelation caused me to watch this news report with newfound interest and to pay attention to the fact that, other than those news reports, no one else on the TV looked like me. Certain things gradually became part of my awareness, just as you learn that a stove is hot and that you have to look both ways before crossing the street. I learned that when we traveled south from our home in West Virginia, we could not assume that restroom facilities at gas stations and other public accommodations were at our disposal. I learned that our White neighbors across the road that ran up the little hollow in which we lived did not want us to play with their grandchildren. I learned that you did not want to be out in certain parts of the county after dark. Just driving your car through the neighborhood could get you in trouble—just because you were Black.

Some wonderful things stood in contradiction to those negative realities. My father's role as a pastor meant that I was exposed to godly men and women of my race. So what if some of them could not read or write? They could pray up a storm, and they could quote the Bible to a degree I have yet to achieve. I grew up fourteen miles outside of Charleston, West Virginia, in a semi-rural setting where I could tramp through the woods. I watched my older brothers put up a basketball goal in our graveled driveway, build dams in the creek that swept past our house, and build a tree house and a fort on the vacant land on the hill above our home. My brother, Rocky, would build roads in the crawl space under the house and under the kitchen porch. It was a rather idyllic childhood when I was in those contexts.

This duality in my existence did not stop there. When I began public school in 1966 after a year of a private, predominantly Black kindergarten, my parents enrolled my older sister and me in Mound Elementary. The school was perched in a residential neighborhood atop an old Indian burial mound. It just wasn't our neighborhood. As a matter of fact, we were the first Black children to ever attend that school. My sister had attended three years at the supposedly integrated but predominantly Black Shawnee Elementary. My mother concluded it was not the best environment, which was borne out by the fact that a couple of years later the school board closed the school, bussing its students to predominantly White schools.

Our entry to Mound Elementary was uneventful. There were no lines of protestors, no need for the National Guard. My dad dropped us off in front of the squatty, two-story brick structure. The square pillars framing the stairs up to the school seemed oh, so impressive to me. I only had one problem there in my first several months, and it occurred on my first day, when an older, poorly kept White kid called me a *nigger* in the bathroom. It stung, but my upbringing and my instincts told me his opinion was not one with which to be overly concerned. As long as he did not threaten me physically, I was OK.

I proceeded to fall in love with school. Learning and books were fascinating to me. I wanted to know more and more. I found myself in a combined first and second grade class and quickly advanced with the small group of first graders who were studying the lessons of the second-grade students. We were all proud when our teacher, Mrs. Mollohan, was named teacher of the year in West Virginia. The photographer from the state publication came to our school and took pictures of the classroom. I was particularly pleased that Mrs. Mollohan had him take pictures of me beside a poster I had made as part of a special project and was proud of my inclusion in the shot of the advanced first graders she was teaching. We all looked forward with anticipation to the publication of the article recognizing her achievement.

My eagerness turned to confusion when the article appeared. They had chosen not to use the photo of me by myself, but they had printed the photo of her advanced first grade students. However, I wasn't there. On closer inspection, I noticed that you could see my knee. They had cropped me (and only me) off the edge of the print. That stung. In retrospect, I realized the photographer must have intentionally orchestrated the shot to leave himself with a "salvageable" image for his article.

Neither do I remember my parents' words of comfort on that occasion. My father was usually pretty silent in such situations, and my mother probably related some version of, "Well, you know, in order to be viewed as equal, you have to be better." This mandate was not a particular burden to me in school, as I was one of the best students in my grade. But, that challenge echoes in my ears and in that of many middle-class African Americans to this day.

I had another, similarly painful experience my first day of junior high. I rode the school bus with the kids from my neighborhood, which in itself was an experience. The conversations and activities on the bus were not always wholesome. It was actually a pretty dangerous ride physically and definitely hazardous emotionally. We were all Black, so it wasn't a racial thing; just the cruelty of teenage boys and girls. Nevertheless, it was nice to be going to school with people from my own neighborhood at last.

As we emerged from the bus, something felt very odd. Some White kids were already there, presumably because they walked to school or were driven there. It really gave me the sense that this was their school and we were being bused in, even though there was no other junior high to go to and we had only traveled a couple of miles. What was even more puzzling was the reaction of the White kids I had gone to school with for six years. They did not seem to see me. As our busload of Black kids walked in, I tried to speak to the friends I had made at Mound Elementary, but they did not reply. It was completely befuddling to me, and left me feeling very much like "a Black kid." There was a bit of a sting at being ignored, but I took comfort in the camaraderie that I had with my bus mates. We were all being ignored or stared at in a bewildered, anxious sort of way. The experience made clear to which group I was really connected.

It wasn't until high school that I read Ralph Ellison's novel *Invisible Man* and recognized that my White friends' response was a part of a broader phenomenon. Ellison poignantly describes the pain of being an object of scorn, pity, fear, and condescending charity, and how in that experience his humanity, individuality, and unique personality were essentially invisible to the broader, controlling White society. They had not responded because they had not "seen me." I was just another Black kid, walking with a group of Black kids. We were "other," invaders, in our afros, bell-bottoms, and neighborhood slang. Their fear clouded their vision, blinding them to the presence of their old elementary school friend.

When the class schedule began, I walked into the advanced classes with many of my elementary school White friends and very few of my Black friends. Once in those classes, my Mound Elementary classmates could "see me" again. I put this observation in my personal mental vault, and we carried on as in times past.

Things had changed some since I was cut out of the picture for the newspaper. Back then, the very idea that a Black child could be in view in the class of a "teacher of the year" was seen as repugnant and probably controversial. By the time I had reached junior high, such blatant disregard was no longer acceptable, but my classmates were still most comfortable relating to me when I was in their world, relating to them in the idioms and terms of their culture. When my "Blackness" was on display, I became just another representative of a rival group, prompting a blindness that preserved the comfort of my White classmates.

∽

Twelve years later, our effort at Howard to create an environment at the fall retreat where Black and White students interacted as peers ran afoul of these same dynamics. For the White students at the fall retreat, when the Howard University delegation's numbers were low enough that we were not affecting the culture of the event, when the White students' music was dominating the cabins and the retreat sessions, all was well; we were forced to blend in. But once those things began to shift, tensions mounted.

4
WHAT ABOUT THE COMMUNITY?

Another point of cultural disconnect for our work at Howard was our living out the Campus Crusade for Christ slogan coined by its cofounder, Dr. Bill Bright: "Reach the campus for Christ today, reach the world for Christ tomorrow." The idea of targeting the future leaders of a society was nothing new. Its application to college students by a Christian organization was a bit of an innovation. The Black leaders within Campus Crusade for Christ always talked about how our vision included the community. However, the philosophy and practice of Campus Crusade for Christ ran counter to that idea. I don't believe it was an intentional devaluation of that arena of ministry, but by the time I came along, the pattern within Campus Crusade for Christ was to reach leaders on the campus and mobilize those leaders to go to the world. There was very little vision cast or strategy developed to reach out holistically to non-students in this country. I realize now that, as a result, we created very few opportunities for students to act on their aspirations to bring about change in the African-American community.

Campus Crusade for Christ's Intercultural Resources (ICR) had once pioneered inner-city summer mission opportunities. When I met Thomas Fritz at the Wildwood, New Jersey, summer mission project, he was there to observe that effort in anticipation of leading a similar one in Washington, DC, the following summer. The DC summer mission project continued for four successive summers, yet our manpower in ICR proved to be insufficient to sustain the effort.

After the 1984 team arrived in the District of Columbia to pioneer the work at Howard, we discontinued the summer project. In the meantime, Here's Life Inner City had been launched as a Campus Crusade ministry to urban communities. Here's Life Inner City (HLIC) operates with a strong passion for the poor, seeking to network those who have means in metropolitan areas with communities and programs within the urban centers that are in need. That usually means suburban White churches connecting with Christian compassion ministries in the inner city. HLIC had seen the success of the ICR inner-city summer mission projects and adopted the approach as a major strategy. Their paradigm mobilized students, White or Black, to engage the needs of the city.

As they developed their Summer in the City missions programs, recruiting students at Campus Crusade Christmas conferences, the overwhelming majority of their participants were White. The hope of the Here's Life Inner City Movement was that their projects would be racially diverse, and their request of us was to send leaders and students to help make that a reality. However, though we sent students and staff to those projects year after year, we struggled to see momentum and growth in Black student participation.

As this continued, I would talk with some of the Black students who attended a Summer in the City project. They would relate that it was a good experience, but they would seldom talk about returning, nor did they actively recruit others to attend. Their stories revolved around their interaction with the White students on the project and how God had used that to grow their patience, love, compassion, and conflict resolution skills.

As I reflected on what was happening to our students, I realized that they were going on these projects to address needs in the Black community but found themselves forced to take on another agenda. During those summers, they lived and served on multi-cultural teams. The White students generally assumed that the Black students had greater insight regarding the cultural exposure they were receiving while on the project. So, despite the reality that many of these Black students were from suburban backgrounds and were on a learning curve of their own, the Black students tended to function as "cultural tour guides."

There are people who are called to such a ministry and others who gravitate to it for less than noble reasons. (One can make a good living by being a cultural tour guide.) But my observation is that Black students who have a passion for the African-American community do not always feel called to get more Whites to understand or become engaged with those needs in order to bring about solutions for the problems in the community. We want to engage those challenges in a way that preserves the dignity and respect of those we are serving and conduct ourselves in a way that produces a healthy, whole community. We want to create pathways for more African-American leaders, college students, and others, to be in a position to make a difference in the lives of those who need inspiration, motivation, or real help.

Even as this was becoming more and more clear, those of us who were focused on Black students in the campus ministry of Campus Crusade for Christ were not providing adequate opportunities for Black students to act on the community component of our vision. As a matter of fact, when a student would express an interest in helping us engage a more community-based ministry, we would often discourage that interest. Our reasoning was that our strategy on campus required ten to fifteen hours per week from students who were committed to our movement. When you add that to their studies and whatever work-study job they may have had, we knew they would not have the where-withal to do all of those things well. Our experience indicated that they would choose the community-based ministry over Campus Crusade and be lost to our effort. Our response was to guard against that happening by counseling them away from acting on a passion for the community. In retrospect, that was a regrettable choice. I was seeking to demonstrate our ministry success in terms that Campus Crusade valued. Our response to the students was consistent with what I had seen and heard within a Campus Crusade campus ministry context. But that approach undermined the motivation of many of the students with whom we were working.

At that time, the lack of engagement of the campus ministry of Campus Crusade for Christ with a community ministry was relatively comfortable for White students. For Black students, that separation was never easy. Perhaps due to the smaller nature of the Black community, perhaps due to the value of extended family, Black students feel a strong sense of pull toward community. Black folk tend not to feel the luxury of dissociating themselves from the community with which they identify. For emerging Black Christian leaders this is a constant tension. When you are exposed to training, education, or other enriching experiences, it pulls you away from those who don't have those opportunities. There are things about those environments, whether the traditional ghettoes or venerable Black institutions, that we may no longer care to be associated with. In some cases, those settings are downright dangerous. Yet, those are the very people who most need our help. In my own life, back when I was a teen I found myself being exposed to and drawn toward two different Black worlds. Navigating that terrain was an unspoken mystery, an unacknowledged maze of choices and opportunities. The wrong turn could lead you into a seemingly inescapable trap. The ground beneath your feet was unstable, and seemed to shift to place you in one hazard after another. I did not always know how to navigate the duality of that terrain, but I felt I was the rope in a tug of war between different futures.

As a kid, I lived on Finney Hollow Road alongside a small creek. On the top of the hill overlooking the hollow was one of the toniest Black neighborhoods in the area, Pinewood Park. It had been given a rather uninspired nickname, "the Hill." Doctor Nelson, Lawyer Lonesome, and other Black professionals and business owners lived there. The children from those homes walked down the hill and past my house to catch the school bus. Across the highway on which we caught the bus was "the Bottom." The Bottom was not a tony neighborhood. The Bottom was called that because it was low-lying land, not far from the river. The folks who lived there were not all poor, but many were.

That separation of the prosperous from the poor was not unusual as the sixties wore into the seventies. It describes a problem that has grown and left the Black community in need of a strategy to connect these two demographics. How can the values, attitudes, skills, and abilities of the Black middle class be used to benefit those being left behind when we flee the Bottom to live on the Hill? Growing up, I was just trying to figure out how to make my own way. Now I see how that experience was a foreshadowing of the calling God would place on my life.

The location of my house meant I was not actually a part of the Pinewood Hill crowd, nor of the Bottom crew. I felt somewhat apart from both. In school, some of my classes were advanced, like pre-algebra, and others were with everyone else. In pre-algebra, I was with many of my Mound Elementary classmates, but my football, basketball, and track friends were mostly Black.

I recall visiting the home of a guy named Red. He was poor, very poor, but he had a collection of over twenty pairs of suede Converse All-Stars. They were the most expensive basketball shoes available at the time. Obviously, they were not from the local shoe store. Later that year, someone stole my watch from my basketball locker. The only person seen entering or leaving the locker room was Red. I chose not to make a big deal of it because I did not want to see my friend sent to juvenile hall, since everyone knew he was one infraction away from matriculating there.

My best friend was Monty Leonard. He and his sister, Betty, had joined my sisters and me at Mound Elementary after a couple of years. We carpooled, which kept us from having to catch the city bus. Monty's father was a detective lieutenant on the Charleston police department and a little league baseball coach. They lived in Pinewood Park, on the Hill. I spent many an hour hanging out in Monty's basement.

A more casual friend of mine was Nick. Nick was built like a dark chocolate battering ram, already a man in the seventh grade, and he was predictably the best football player in our class. Nick lived in the Bottom, and his parents were no longer together, although his father would sometimes give us rides to our away football games. His dad drove the nicest, flashiest Cadillac I had ever seen. They called him "Candyman." Nick tried hard in school, but he did not have the foundation to do well. I tried to help him once when one of the kids made a mistake grading Nick's English test. Nick needed all the points he could get, so I went to the teacher on his behalf. The teacher would not even consider my petition to get Nick's grade improved. I don't know what her deal was, but I could not help but feel that if it had been some White kid, she would have heard me out. A few weeks after Nick's dad had given us a ride to a game, I saw an article on the front page of the Charleston Gazette. Detective Ed Leonard (Monty's father) was shown displaying the drugs occupying the space in the trunk of the Cadillac I had been in not that long ago. He had busted the Candyman. Those drugs were sitting in the same space where my football gear had been just a few days before. It turned out that Nick's father was the biggest drug dealer in town.

This juxtaposition of realities is what we, as Black people, face. We see our friends and compatriots struggling to make it. Those of us who are blessed with some ability or have had better opportunities find ourselves stymied when we try to reach out and help, like I felt when I tried to help Nick. It seems that too many things are not in our control. We discover that we are only one relationship away, one decision away from falling on the wrong side of the law, the economy, the moral morass that threatens to derail our positive aspirations. As time goes on, just as my class schedule limited my contact with most of the Black students in my junior high school, middle and upper-middle class opportunities, whether in employment or housing, remove us from the people who can most benefit from being exposed to our leadership. Campus Crusade's methodology at the time simply made the separation more acute.

5
THE MOTHERLAND IS WAITING

CONCURRENT TO THESE developments in our ministry at Howard was a steady awakening to the ministry needs and opportunities in Africa. I had taken African American and African history courses as an undergrad. When I had served under Thomas Fritz, the patriarch of the Black campus ministry of Campus Crusade for Christ, he talked about the time he went to Africa and the people asked him, "Where are the Negro Christians from America? We never see them. Only the Whites." He related how these encounters fueled his passion to see a movement raised up to change our community and to help take the gospel to the world.

Ministering at Howard forced me to take my African history knowledge to another level. Afrocentrism, that reaction to the Eurocentric nature of education in the United States that seeks to place African history and cultures at the center of one's thinking, philosophy, and values, was strong on the campus. It was so strong that every third year the Howard University Student Association president possessed a strongly Afrocentric persona, whether a sympathizer with the Nation of Islam or some other Afrocentric ideology. The cyclical pattern was that the year after the Black nationalist's administration, a vocal Christian would win the subsequent election, followed in turn by a business-oriented student. There would be a backlash against the Western image provided by the corporate look of that president and a fairly radical Afrocentrist would win the subsequent election. Then, the cycle would begin again.

In 1986, Thomas Fritz recommended me to be a part of Campus Crusade for Christ's University Ministry Training Conference, held in Harare, Zimbabwe. I was honored to be asked to serve in this way, given I had only completed two years in my role as campus director and our ministry was just getting started.

It was an eye-opening time. Our itinerary took us through Amsterdam, which was my first exposure to Europe. The age of the place struck me, as did the apparent gathering of wealth from distant lands. I don't know how I could tell. Most of the people I met were simple, decent folks. But, they were all multilingual, and there were lots of African and Middle Eastern immigrants. On a tour of the canals, we saw ancient brownstone homes, left vacant by their vacationing occupants, but which spoke of generational wealth.

As we continued, our overnight flight greeted the dawn as our flight path gave us a view of the Nile River Valley. The majesty of that river, and the irony of its arid surroundings struck me. I wept over seeing for the first time the continent of my ancestors and thinking of all the biblical history that had taken place within those lands.

My traveling partner, Emory Davis, and I were to spend a week before the training conference getting "on the ground" exposure to the campus ministry in Malawi. During a transit stop in Nairobi a customs officer pelted us with what seemed to be bribe-inviting questions, claiming that Emory's luggage could not be found. Eventually he relented without us offering any cash. Emory's luggage mysteriously appeared, and we boarded an Air Malawi flight to Lilongwe. The entire flight crew was black, a first in my experience, and while the plane made me nervous, the service was courteous, efficient and warm. Upon our arrival, we met our host, Lot Dzonzi, a recent university graduate who had turned down a post in his country's foreign service to be a missionary to college students, much like Emory and me. He hosted us in his humble concrete-block home structure, whose windows had no panes. We slept under mosquito netting to avoid contracting the malaria that Lot periodically battled. Lot's cook, a local man, prepared us a breakfast of a boiled egg and a corn meal paste, not unlike grits. I relished the two-mile walk down the road to and from campus with Lot. As we walked, he would fill our ears with tales of his country, the ministry there, and the nature of the culture. I gained a greater appreciation for Jesus' teaching of the disciples as they walked "along the way."

Lot's descriptions of his country stirred many feelings of a kinship in our respective cultures. Dating practices, in which a representative of a young man's family would speak to a representative of a young lady's family to see if such a match would be acceptable, reminded me of the practices of African-American youth before integration. In the U.S., a friend replaced the family member as the mediator between the families. But the use of proxies or ambassadors was still a part of our culture. Those practices have eroded since desegregation, and while it may be difficult to document the cultural connection, I believe it exists.

Less tenuous were my observations of the musical influences of Africa in African-American culture. I sat in a student-led prayer meeting on campus and participated as the leader used a call-and-response style to prompt us in singing the common praise chorus, "Father, I Adore You." While the song was a product of the White American Christian folk music phenomenon, as the Africans sang it, I was more comfortable than when I had heard the song sung in the U.S. Not only that, but some of the women were singing in a nasal sort of soprano in which I had never heard White people sing. It reminded me of Mrs. White, one of the mothers of the church in which I grew up. Academicians have documented the rhythms and cadences, musical scales and antiphonal traditions of Africa in African-American music traditions. Yet, this simple style of singing was what produced in me the strongest sense of connection with the people of Africa.

On the other hand, the people of Malawi were also fascinated with Emory and me. When we went to the bank to exchange some money, the security guard approached us and said, "Are you from America?"

"Yes."

With some quizzical skepticism, he asked if he could see a penny, which we readily produced for his inspection. His face lit up, he began to speak to other bank workers in his own language, and they all began to react with interest and welcome. This has been my experience everywhere I travel in Africa, more so in small towns than in the cities, where Black Americans are more likely to have traveled.

Of course, there are those we encounter in Africa who see us as a potential payday, but I cannot blame them. Even as a missionary, I make an amount that would place me in a very well-off position in most African countries. White people in Africa often do not understand or appreciate the affinity Africans in Africa feel for African Americans. On that first trip to Malawi, we attended a staff retreat with Campus Crusade for Christ. There were a handful of Malawian staff members and an even smaller number of White missionaries in attendance. As Emory and I shared the warm reception we were experiencing, one of the White missionaries, who had not spent a lot of time in Africa, began to question the value of African Americans serving as missionaries in Malawi. I was initially surprised that he would presume to have an opinion on the subject, but I was comforted when the Malawian staff quickly corrected his perception. Long-term American missionary Bill Beauvais, also

White, spoke of the value of African Americans coming to the continent.

When we arrived in Zimbabwe for the conference, we stayed at the Mandel Training Center. The country was only a few years into independence under liberation-fighter-cum-president Robert Mugabe. The military presence in the country was more pervasive than anywhere I had been before, and the frequent use of the word *comrade* was a new experience. The potential of the country was apparent, and I grieve the painful paroxysms it continues to undergo.

While at the conference, I was befriended by many of the African leaders in attendance. One, a Reverend Mpayo from Tanzania, sat me down at a meal and pleaded with me to send other Black missionaries. He went on to describe the growing backlash of resentment among educated Africans toward the West and western missionaries.

"You are our kin," he said. "We want to hear from you, to see you, to know what you have to say. When you bring us the message of Christ, many of the objections of the people are swept away. I have been to your country. I know that millions of Black Americans are Christians. But we know nothing of you in our land." He made me promise to come myself or to send others. While we have sent hundreds to various countries as short-term missionaries, I have yet to fulfill the promise I made in 1986 to visit Tanzania.

I left my time in Africa with several deep and lasting impressions. I did not feel called to be a long-term missionary in Africa. I did feel a broadened sense of purpose. First of all, I understood Black American culture in a way I had not before. As a result, I understood myself better. Some of the ways that we African Americans feel that we are peculiar are not peculiar at all in Africa, from our cyclical view of time (lateness is tolerated as a reflection of a more relational approach to encounters) to the understanding that when visiting it is impolite to refuse food or refreshment.

When, as newlyweds, Rebecca and I went to Mamou, Louisiana, for me to get to know her grandparents and other extended family members, she emphatically explained to me that I must not eat much at any one home. When offered food, I was to say, "Oh, I am so full. But that looks so good, I will take a little." After eating, if offered seconds, good manners required that I accept. This had to be my conduct in every home we visited—and we visited several—if I wanted to avoid being known as "the uppity northern Negro." This briefing is remarkably similar to ones I have received when traveling in Africa.

The "Africanisms" in African-American culture of which the scholars speak are quite real. I left that trip believing, as I still do, that to be well-educated, an African American needs to travel to Africa. Otherwise that person's appreciation of their own culture, their ability to appraise its strengths and weaknesses, will be weak. I also felt stirring in me an awareness that brings together several elements from my formative years.

I believe the name of the church some of my ancestors helped establish in Malden, West Virginia, is significant: African Zion Baptist Church. That church was founded in 1857 in what was then Virginia, a slave state. My Christian forefathers had a sense of Africa being our Zion. This strain of thought runs throughout the writings of early African-American Christians. Their hearts yearned to take the gospel back to the continent of their (or their parents') birth. Many dreamed of returning to Africa as Marcus Garvey's early twentieth-century "Back to Africa" movement demonstrated. Yet, God in His sovereignty had not allowed that repatriation to happen in significant numbers. Like the ancient Hebrews in Egypt, we had grown numerous and, in these latter days, prosperous. Could there be a Joseph story taking shape among us? The thought of reestablishing an active connection to

Africa lay somewhat dormant in me, only to be awakened some years later.

There was an attempt to capture and capitalize on this missionary zeal during the 1980s. Crawford Loritts, the highest ranking African American on Campus Crusade for Christ staff, and Dr. Elward Ellis, the leading African American at Inter-Varsity Christian Fellowship, joined forces to lead Destiny '87, a conference designed to rally African Americans for the cause of world evangelization. The conference was well attended, drawing some two thousand attendees, but was left with financial challenges. One more Destiny conference was held, but the organization that was envisioned never got off the ground.

The Destiny Movement's failure to survive is a cautionary tale. The desire to develop a para-church ministry that focuses on African Americans in not new. There were other attempts to do so, as well. Harambee, another Campus Crusade for Christ spinoff, was attempted in the 1970s. Tom Skinner Associates at one point launched a variety of ministries, including a college campus component. It still exists as the Skinner Leadership Institute, one of the few non-church-based Christian organizations founded and led by African Americans. The challenge such an organization faces is multi-faceted, but hinges on whether there is enough will in the Black community to fund such an effort and whether there is enough value of the work such an organization can accomplish that it attracts resources from outside the Black community.

6

THE EMERGENCE OF A MOVEMENT

Impact '91

CONFERENCES PROVIDED CRITICAL motivation, challenge, and vision in all of my ministry experience. Just a few weeks after Rebecca and I completed our initial fund development time and moved to Atlanta, with her eight months pregnant, we were off to Chicago for Chicago '81. Chicago '81 was a national gathering of African-American students, laymen, and pastors. Its organizers intended to cast vision for and provide training in strategies to reach our community and mobilize laborers for a worldwide harvest of souls. The theme was "A Critical Moment in Black America." Crawford Loritts led the charge, supported by Thomas Fritz, Haman Cross, and Pastor Willie Richardson. Loritts issued a challenge to join him in believing God for five hundred laborers to be sent as missionaries to help fulfill the Great Commission. The conference was inspiring. I will never forget the day of outreach at that conference. That day the high was twenty degrees, and it snowed. I was moved to see nearly three thousand young Black people standing in line around the block to board the elevated trains to share their faith in the various neighborhoods of Chicago that day.

The messages were stirring as well, including a cameo appearance by Rev. Jesse Jackson and an unforgettable sermon by Dr. E. V. Hill from Los Angeles. He spoke of the despair many in the Black community felt when Ronald Reagan (who Dr. Hill supported) was elected president. He said, "No more food stamps, no more welfare, no more this, no more that, but wait a minute...there is God!" Many report the significance of the conference in their lives. Hearing the testimony of actual African-American missionaries and that of Rev. Siphu Bengu from South Africa was transforming.

Within Campus Crusade for Christ in the years after Chicago '81, Tom Fritz began to try to supplement the Black student ministry by hosting an annual Black Student Leadership Conference in the spring, initially piggybacking off of Howard's annual spring break trip to Florida. As the years went on, the event landed on the Martin Luther King holiday weekend. These were small conferences, perhaps 120 or so in attendance, but were nonetheless significant in the lives of the students. These Black student leadership conferences attracted a variety of students who were involved in Campus Crusade for Christ.

The dynamic of being involved with Campus Crusade for Christ was particularly problematic for the students who were returning to predominantly White campuses. As we engaged several waves of these students, several broad categories of students emerged. There were those who had not had a heavily Black experience. They may have attended predominantly White schools all their lives, lived in White suburbs, and were naturally comfortable within Campus Crusade for Christ. Some of these folks were brought to the event by White CCC staff members who wanted to encourage them to reach out to other African-American students. There were those who had grown up with a significant connection to the Black community but in the process of their encounter with Campus Crusade were drifting away from their neighborhood, church, or other connections. Many of them found themselves attending a White church, fellowshiping with White Christians, and often developing a judgmental disdain for Black culture in general and the Black church in particular. Then there were those who were receiving some benefit from their CCC involvement but were determined to remain connected to the Black community. This type of student often continued to attend a Black church and participate in Black organizations on campus. Usually, they would attend one or two CCC events and then fade from the scene. Few would stick around long enough to consider joining those of us who were committed to reaching the Black community as a part of Campus Crusade for Christ.

In 1988, CCC's ad hoc committee for African-American ministry (called the InterCultural Resources [ICR] Task Force) assembled again to pray and plan for how we could move forward. These meetings were held annually, and I had participated since I was named director of the work at Howard. This time there was a spirit of desperation as we prayed and wept in recognition and grief of the fact that we were losing a battle of attrition. Students were joining our staff at a trickle that was not keeping up with the outflow of African Americans who felt that raising support was just too difficult, were frustrated with the insensitivity or ignorance of their leadership, or who sensed a call to some other ministry.

In December of that school year, Tom Fritz visited the Campus Crusade for Christ Christmas conference in Philadelphia, to which our Howard University team had attempted to recruit student attendees to little avail. While there, we talked about the need to host another national event like Chicago '81 to call students to a vision for spiritual change. At our ICR Task Force meeting in 1989, Tom tried to rally us to have a national conference. Though I was in favor of it, several of the group felt we did not have the manpower to pull off something that big. We tabled the idea until the next year. The 1990 meeting began with a recognition that we were in an even worse position to organize a national conference, yet Tom persisted in challenging us to consider it. Marcella Charles and Gladys Hillman encouraged us to pray about it, and after a season of prayer, the group decided to move forward. The conference was named "Impact '91: A Cry of Hope, a Call to Action." God was about to shake things up. My life and my ministry would never be the same.

The conference was the beginning of a new day. Tom Fritz drove the planning process with the help of Kevin Werst, a White staff member who had graduated from one of the bastions of Campus Crusade's campus ministry, Miami University in Oxford, Ohio. Kevin had served with Crawford Loritts for several years in the 1980s. He was an administrative genius who coordinated this major effort on a shoestring and ended the process with a positive balance. I was program director, as well as one of the main session speakers. The conference drew well over five hundred people. The dynamic was compelling, the camaraderie intense, and the training vintage Campus Crusade for Christ with a heavy dose of rhetoric about community concern. We talked of passing on the baton, and Tom Fritz and others passed a symbolic baton-like scrolled document out to the attendees on New Year's Eve.

The program for the event was conceived with one limitation. We knew that our overall agenda was to send these students back to engage in Campus Crusade for Christ on their respective campuses. So, we chose to program the conference to reflect a cultural middle ground. We were concerned that if we had speakers and musicians who sounded too Black, our students would be discontent when they returned to the White world of Campus Crusade for Christ. However, the students did not receive this limitation. The conference was held in what was then the Airport Sheraton, which was connected to the Georgia International Convention Center. One night Tom Fritz and I were up late planning or talking and stood on the balcony overlooking the lobby below. There were over one hundred students gathered around the baby grand piano singing contemporary urban gospel music under the enthusiastic direction of Russell Hardeman, the student leader of the ministry at Jackson State University in Mississippi. They were energized by the experience, sounded quite good, and were enjoying themselves into the wee hours of the morning. The songs they were singing were even more powerfully consistent with the message and theme of the conference than that which our accomplished African-American evangelical crossover artists were delivering in the main meeting. Some of the students did not sleep at all. Tom and I looked at each other as we leaned over the balcony railing and said, "You think God is trying to tell us something?" We agreed that night not to try and massage the program of the next conference to make it "less Black." We would program a conference that would speak the heart language of the African-American student. Dennis Talbert, youth pastor at Rosedale Park Baptist Church in Detroit, pastored by Rev. Haman Cross, was adamant that we must do this event again. He agreed to volunteer his own time and expertise to make it happen.

Our original intent had been to host the event every three years to give Campus Crusade for Christ Christmas conferences a chance to capitalize on the momentum from the Impact conferences. This would also keep us from exhausting our staff and avoided a head-to-head conflict with InterVarsity Christian Fellowship's Black student conference. InterVarsity's conference was on an every-three-year cycle to avoid competition with IV's premier missions conference, "Urbana," which was also on an every-three-year-cycle. So, we set our sights on Impact '94. But some things began to change around us. Campus Crusade for Christ had a new national campus director, Steve Sellers, and he was about to start a process to transform that ministry.

MARLA'S STORY

Being an academician of faith is one thing, being an *anthropologist* of faith is quite another! In countless ways I attribute the consistent and biblically grounded ministry of Impact with my uncompromising faith in the Lordship of Jesus Christ. In the midst of daunting questions and challenging life circumstances, the simple truths of Christ continue to resonate with me because of the foundation that was laid while I was an undergraduate at Spelman College.

Through weekly Bible studies and amazing regional and national seminars I learned to appreciate the "meat" of the gospel. I attended the first Impact conference in 1991, then in 1994, then again in 1996! Beyond the seminars, however (because great preaching is a profitable industry these days), we were discipled by Impact staff members whose lives reflected genuine transformation, whose commitment to integrity made them easy to follow, and whose humility allowed us to walk closely beside them and see very transparently their different journeys with the Lord.

Beyond the words shared in one hundred Bible studies and one thousand speeches, their lives left an indelible imprint on my life. They love their families, honor their spouses, pray for their friends and communities, and care for the least of these. They petitioned us to follow them as they followed Christ, and I am altogether a better Christian because of it.

—MARLA FREDERICK, PhD
ASSOCIATE PROFESSOR OF AFRICAN AND
AFRICAN AMERICAN STUDIES
AND OF THE STUDY OF RELIGION
HARVARD UNIVERSITY

Personally, the year leading up to Impact '91 was a tough one. There was a restlessness in me that I had difficulty explaining. We were seeing great things happen at Howard, but I was wrestling with two deeply troubling realities. In terms of the mission, we were seeing everything we hoped for happen at Howard, except for one critical disappointment. Virtually no students were joining us in our effort to raise up a Black student movement as a part of Campus Crusade for Christ. Many highly gifted people were coming to know Christ. These individuals were going to lead in the future. Yet, despite our thoughtfully planned and carefully executed strategies—not to mention a number of personal and impassioned pleas—we were seeing too few graduating students join with us as staff. This was a national phenomenon, but we had hoped to be able to experience a different reality at Howard. Regretfully, it was not to be.

This was particularly devastating, given the methodology we had invested in as a part of Campus Crusade for Christ. That methodology required the assigning of staff teams to individual campuses in order to raise up, build, and maintain a movement on that campus. We were not seeing enough people join to maintain the locations we had established (Howard, Jackson State, and the schools of the Atlanta University Center), much less to expand to be able to reach Black students across the country.

On top of this frustration, I experienced persistent and growing problems in the financial support of our ministry, which meant that our family's finances were not in order. After the initial season, in which we saw a rapid response to our invitations to join our group of regular financial backers, we settled into an experience much more typical for African-American missionaries. A number of our Black donors were new to this style of supporting missionaries. They were more accustomed to channeling their giving through their local church. The idea of writing a monthly check seemed to connect with some but not with most. After a few years, it became clear that there were both individuals and churches who would only give when they saw us face to face. Our White donor base was more consistent but less connected with what we were trying to do. There are notable exceptions, like Perrow Presbyterian Church in West Virginia, which has been with us since 1981, and Tenth Presbyterian Church in Philadelphia, which has stuck with us for two decades. Our largest individual supporters have tended to be White. Yet, our goal remains to see the majority of our funding come from the African-American community.

The cost of living in the nation's capital exacerbated our difficulty with funding. We struggled there despite the fact that some of the most prosperous Black folk in the country are in the DC area. However, as Harlem Renaissance writer Langston Hughes noted in his day, the Black community in DC is often more consumed by appearing prosperous than actually being prosperous. Our efforts to secure funding from the African-American community in DC never were able to keep up with our needs. I served as part of the ministerial staff at Nineteenth Street Baptist Church, one of the most prominent older churches in the city, with doctors, attorneys, retired generals, and the like, yet our endeavors to tap that well of relationships was often futile. We did eventually manage to buy a home in DC through the District's Housing Purchase Assistance Program. The District of Columbia declared us the one-thousandth homebuyer and featured us as such at a press conference with then-Mayor Marion Barry. But, with a growing family (Caleb, our fifth child was born in June 1991) and a collapsing public school system in DC, we could not see how we could afford to remain in ministry there.

I concluded that Rebecca and I had done all that we could do to raise up this national movement from a Howard University base and that there was no better base in the Black community. I reasoned if we were ever going to be able to sustain a Black student movement as a part of Campus Crusade for Christ, things needed to change at the structural level, and that if they were not going to change, I needed to prepare myself for the next step in ministry. Several of our friends, including Marc Anthony in Atlanta and Grover Cooper in Jackson, had reached similar conclusions and were taking their families overseas— Marc to France to reach francophone Africans there and Grover to South Africa. If they could not get others to go to the mission field, they and their families would go themselves.

At Rebecca's urging, I wanted to get some seminary training in order to write more compellingly and decided to attend Reformed Theological Seminary in Orlando. I figured that I could carve out a role of some sort representing InterCultural Resources as a part of the national campus office there and hopefully affect some change. If not, well, at least I would be prepared to find another vehicle to live out the calling God had placed on my life. I announced my impending departure and many fond farewells were given. Not only were Rebecca and I leaving, but Marcella Charles was also leaving to go to seminary, and James and Cynthia White were moving to North Carolina to be a part of Campus Crusade for Christ's communication center. Melvita Chisolm and Janice Johnson would remain at Howard to carry on the ministry.

In the meantime, Steve Sellers, in his new role as National Director of the Campus Ministry in the U.S., was formulating plans to change that ministry in profound ways. The campus ministry of Campus Crusade for Christ was and is the core of the organization. Campus Crusade for Christ started on the campus of UCLA, and much of its genius has been its effectiveness at reaching and mobilizing emerging leaders for the cause of Christ, both in this country and abroad. However, from 1974–1992, the campus ministry in the U.S. had been in a season of stagnation; some would even call it a decline. The U.S. Campus Ministry was the wellspring of much of Campus Crusade for Christ's global expansion, yet the reach and effectiveness of the ministry in this country had not appreciably improved since the early 1970s.

During our final school year at Howard, rumblings of major changes began to course through the Campus Crusade grapevine. As things unfolded, my leaders, Jim Keller and Mike Tilley, were asked to move to Florida to be a part of the new national leadership team of the campus ministry. Regional offices were eliminated, and the twenty-one area offices were being consolidated into ten. As this developed, I was asked to participate in a research and development project taking place in Colorado during the summer of 1992. Campus Crusade for Christ holds its national staff conference on the campus of Colorado State University in the summer every two years, but this was not a staff conference summer. Yet, Mike Tilley had recommended me for the research project, so I left For Sale signs in the yard at our Washington, DC, home and took my family to Colorado for the summer. As the time there drew to a close, I spoke with Jim Keller about my aspirations to establish an InterCultural Resources role in the national campus office. He informed me that not only were they prepared to empower that vision but they had been speaking with Tom Fritz about the ultimate objective of all the restructuring—to put things in place and in play to get the gospel to every student. That included ethnic students, and they wanted ICR to be a part of the national leadership in order to lead the entire campus ministry in that effort. I replied, "So Tom is moving to Orlando, too! That is exciting."

Jim replied, "Tom doesn't want to move from Atlanta, so we want you to take the role."

I was a little shocked. I had always assumed Tom Fritz would be my leader in ICR and that I would operate under his auspices. As we talked, Jim explained that it was not his role to offer, and that they wanted to speak with Tom again. I wanted to talk to Tom, too. As I talked with Tom, what emerged was a plan whereby he would take leadership of the non-campus ministry parts of ICR, while I would lead the campus component of it. In that regard, I would lead the next Impact conference. Jim had also mentioned that the ICR role was to lead in reaching every ethnic student, Black, Latino, and Asian. This required a bit more thought and prayer on Rebecca's and my part because of the clarity of our calling. Yet, we felt that much of what we had learned in developing ministry to African Americans would be of benefit to our Asian-American and Latino-American brothers and sisters. It wasn't until a few weeks later, after the project in Colorado was over and we were attending a family reunion in Hilton Head, North Carolina, that I finally got the call from Steve Sellers himself. He said, "We want you to be the national director of InterCultural Resources for the campus ministry, and we want you to move now." Rebecca and I prayed about it overnight and the next day called back to say I would take the role.

The process of engaging the change that Steve Sellers, John Rogers, Mark McCloskey, Dave Sander, and the other architects of the transformation had envisioned was exhilarating. I realized that if what Impact needed to do and become were ever to be possible as a part of or in connection with Campus Crusade for Christ, "the System Change," as it came to be called, had to work. Over the next eleven years, I invested a great deal of energy in seeing that change process succeed. And in a variety of ways, it began to do just that. Steve Douglass, as executive vice president, had sponsored an experiment called Student Linc to serve local campuses over the phone. It had shown great promise, and Mike Tilley and his catalytic ministry team took that strategy and deployed staff across the country to develop ministry in a non-staff-intensive methodology that began to see outstanding fruitfulness. Campus Crusade for Christ's international involvement continued to grow through its worldwide student network, led first by John Rogers and then by Greg and Charmaine Lillestrand.

At the same time as this organizational change was taking place in the campus ministry, we were preparing for Impact '94. As national director of InterCultural Resources for the Campus Ministry, the Impact conference was now under my leadership. Tom and I swapped the roles we played with Impact '91, with him serving as program director and me serving as conference director. Kevin Werst moved his family down to Orlando in 1993 to help us plan the conference. We developed a video to make recruitment of Black conferees easy for White CCC staff. We programmed the conference to speak more fully the language of the African-American college student, opening up the praise and worship for the conference singing John P. Kee's "Jesus Is Real," one of the most popular contemporary gospel songs of that year. The energy in the room was amazing. The speakers were powerful. Over 1,100 people attended.

I was particularly concerned about our New Year's Eve celebration, which we planned to do as a joint session with the Campus Crusade Christmas conference being held around the corner from Impact '94. Our event took place during the heyday of racial reconciliation talk in the White Christian community, fueled by the emergence of Promise Keepers, which made racial reconciliation one of their Seven Promises of a Promise Keeper. I had actually approached Joe Bucha, CCC's southeast regional director for staffed campus ministries, about Impact and the CCC Atlanta regional Christmas conference doing a joint session on New Year's Eve. I thought that if we prayed Daniel 9 together as we prayed in the New Year, perhaps the Lord would heal our land of the consequences of the sins of the generations that preceded ours.

It is my conviction that racial healing in this country will occur best when it is led from the body of Christ. It is problematic that the movement for racial justice that was led from the Black church during the Civil Rights Movement was not embraced widely by the White church until it became the law of the land. This has had many devastating consequences. Daniel's prayer in chapter nine of the book that bears his name can be demonstrated to be the application, by Daniel, of the instruction delineated in Leviticus 26:40–42. The Leviticus passage is the prescription for how God's people are to respond when they find themselves dealing with the consequences of a previous generation's sin. Too many individuals who responded to the call of the racial reconciliation movement refused to engage this biblical mandate.

When we initially informed the Impact students that we were going to "pray in" the New Year with the Campus Crusade Christmas conference, many were resistant to the idea. They asked, "Why do we have to go over to them? We always have to come into their world. Why don't they come into ours for once?" I explained that their meeting room was expandable while ours was not and challenged the group, based on 1 Corinthians 12:21, to engage this expression of our commitment to the unity of the body of Christ. They responded well.

The event was significant but somewhat disappointing. Steve Sellers came, and he and I shared the stage, asking the audience to pray in parallel with Daniel 9. But, the White students were more focused on partying the New Year in than in praying it in. It reinforced the reality that for young White students, racial issues were easy to ignore. Doing business with God over the racial history of this nation was not and is not a high priority for the majority of White students.

Mike Adamson, one of my colleagues on the campus national team noted, "You are different at Impact. You lead in a different way." What he may have been seeing was me relating in the context of the culture that is my own. Up to that point, he had mostly seen me function in the context of the predominantly White leadership venues of Campus Crusade for Christ. At the Impact conference, I was much more at home.

Another White CCC coworker commented, "I felt pretty at ease at Impact '91. I am uncomfortable at Impact '94." Her comment actually gave me a sense of reassurance that we had successfully made the shift toward creating a conference that reflected the culture of the students, not one that occupied a middle ground between that culture and the broader culture of Campus Crusade for Christ.

However, another sentiment I heard during Impact '94 troubled me. One of our strongest allies in Campus Crusade for Christ, a person who had spent major time engaging African-American students, stated, "I am glad we had this conference. Now that we have had it, I don't think another one will be necessary. We can get about the business of making our regional Christmas conferences Black-student-friendly." While I appreciated the heart and aspiration behind the comment, I knew that developing an effective ministry to Black students would not be that simple. After discovering that this idea was fairly widespread among my White comrades in Campus Crusade for Christ, I proposed an experiment. We encouraged each regional Christmas conference to do everything they could to make their conference attractive to African-American students for the December 1995/January 1996 conference season. Rebecca and I, as well as other InterCultural Resources leaders would be available to speak and consult in the planning process. But, I asked the leadership of each conference to do a head count of the number of African Americans present at their event.

The results were startling to some but confirming to us. An aggregate of approximately 110 Black students attended all the regional Christmas conferences. Let me be clear. This was the sum total, not an average. The average attendance was in the range of ten to twenty students per conference, despite the best efforts of the regional Campus Crusade for Christ staff to program and market the conference in a way that would appeal to Black students. The debate was over. While an effort to create an atmosphere within Campus Crusade for Christ in which Black students would feel comfortable was maintained, it moved to second place behind developing strategies and programs that would effectively engage the needs of Black students. We decided to move to an every-other-year timetable for the Impact national conference, making the next national conference Impact '96.

The initial response of White Campus Crusade for Christ staff to the Impact conferences reflected a similar experience I had as a child.

Despite the pains and racism I experienced in the integration of my elementary school, perhaps the worst thing about integrating Mound Elementary was that I did not attend school with kids in my neighborhood. I longed to be able to engage in the after-school baseball, basketball, and football games with my classmates. While Mound was in an adjacent district, it was just far enough away to keep me from riding my bike to the neighborhood more than once or twice during my six years of elementary school. My middle-class family was certainly no worse off than those of my classmates. My father was a pastor and a firefighter; not just a firefighter, but a captain in the Charleston Fire Department. He drove his fire inspector's car home many days. I was no more proud than when he visited the school in full dress uniform for a "teach-in," lecturing our second grade class in fire safety.

There was a lingering sense of alienation, though, which may explain why my favorite place in the school was in the library. I think I read virtually every book in which I was remotely interested. The public library was a frequent haunt. My mother would walk us two hundred yards out to the main highway to catch the city bus fourteen miles to the main county library. When we were little, she would read stories to us at night, sometimes in Spanish, her major in college. As we grew older, she would buy us books through the Scholastic books program and encouraged us to read. I had no greater joy than losing myself in some far-off time or place, experiencing the wonder and intrigue of other lands and cultures, and other people's problems.

My world was a study in contrasts, and I was dealing with adolescence in the midst of navigating the surging swells of integration. My education was taking place in a nearly all-White world. Every other aspect of my existence took place in the Black community, but it was dependent on the wider White world for employment, shopping, medical services, and more. My church was Black, my home life was Black, but when we turned on the TV, Black characters were few and far between. It caused a bit of commotion when *Julia* premiered, featuring the first Black lead, and one that was depicted in a positive, intelligent manner. We admired Bill Cosby's *I Spy* role, as well. In the summers, we would hang around the house until we could go to the summer recreation program at West Virginia State College (now University), the historically Black school only a mile from my home.

My story is not unique. Many of us grew up in families that valued hard work, achievement, and personal responsibility. Yet, the connections and ties that bound the Black community together were strained. Those who had the talent and skills to help lift their fellows from the mire of social and economic marginalization were pulled away from those opportunities. While in elementary school, I had little meaningful contact with my Black peers, except for the hour we sat in Sunday school together.

Lorraine Hansberry's play *A Raisin in the Sun* dramatizes the struggle of the fifties and sixties generation to gain access to better neighborhoods with better schools, more enduring property values, and better community services. The play paints in stark and moving terms the effort that was made to buy off a Black family trying to purchase a home outside the ghetto. They had labored, prayed, scrimped, and saved to be able to do so, yet they were offered even more money to not make that purchase. Yet, that drama—and the success of those who sought to move out of the ghetto—describes an unanticipated tragedy. As Black people left to live in homes that their hard work and responsibility qualified them to purchase, they left behind those who needed to learn from their example. They were no longer in position to give others the opportunity to benefit from the model they presented and experience the value of the knowledge, information, and values gained in that pursuit. Entire neighborhoods were (and still are) left without fathers in the home or without men who held down legal jobs, as all the intact two-income households moved to better digs.

Housing was just one facet of the problem. Institutions of higher learning integrated as well, leaving historically Black colleges and universities in a conundrum. The best students were no longer matriculating at Howard, Hampton, and Fisk. Could these institutions compete with Harvard, Yale, and Princeton, with their billion-dollar endowments?

My story is a classic Black middle-class story. The opportunities that we experienced in the wake of desegregation had the sometimes subtle and sometimes not-so-subtle effect of pulling us away from and out of the communities that originally produced us. A need to prove ourselves drove us. We wanted to demonstrate that we belonged. We had been taught that in order to be viewed as equal, we had to be better, so we sought to master the White man's ways while secretly resenting the devaluation of our own culture and experience implicit in that process. At times, the acculturation process caused us to interpret the world in a manner that was critical of the Black community and Black culture. Some abandoned the Black community altogether, seeking to be "post-racial" before that was practically possible. The result was scores of Black students and young professionals trying to live out the optimism and idealism of the "I Have a Dream" speech. But, when you are learning a foreign culture, looking to prove everyone's assumptions incorrect, looking over your shoulder to ward off the oft-suspected blindside racial attack, it leaves little energy to think about helping those who are not experiencing the opportunities to which you so preciously cling.

The legitimate goal of integrating our society, removing the obstacles to physical, residential, educational, and economic mobility was an admirable, just, and achievable aspiration. However, it has had the unintended effect of leaving those who continue to need help, hope, and inspiration without an adequate source of such support.

In the same way, Campus Crusade's well-intentioned goal of integrating Black students came at a significant cost. While unity in the body is a biblical ideal, that pursuit can reflect an unwillingness to recognize the independent Black spiritual community as legitimate. As we prepared for Impact '96, I simultaneously began seeking to launch parallel strategies for Asian-American students, which became known as "Epic," and for Latino students under the moniker "Destino." Impact '96 became a watershed event in other ways. Kevin and his wife, Patricia, an Italian-American from New York, decided that after more than ten years in ministry to African Americans, it was time to leave and enter the secular workplace. We had lost money on Impact '94, and the planning for Impact '96 was moving at a slow pace. Encouraging signs were the addition of four people—Chris Restuccia, Terry Alexander, Michelle Holliday, and Lisa Hudson—to our team in Orlando. But, as we began 1996, I was beginning to despair of our ability to grow this ministry as a part of Campus Crusade for Christ.

One of the disappointments I had been experiencing was the challenge of raising money for Impact staff and projects. The staff needed help because we were seeing that African-American staff spent a higher percentage of their time working on support than their White counterparts. The median income per capita in the White community is 22 percent higher than in the Black community. One could argue that we Black staff should live on lower incomes than White staff, but that seems morally wrong, given that we go to the same conferences and buy the same gas as our White coworkers. This discrepancy is compounded by the well-documented differences in how Whites and Blacks give. Black folk give a higher percentage of their income than the White community at large, but the bulk of those funds is given to the church and secondarily to educational institutions. The type of philanthropy that fuels the funding base of many White para-church organizations is uncommon in the Black community.

There is an even more devastating factor to be considered, however. The Black community is still beset with a culture of indebtedness that traces its roots back to the sharecropping system in the South and the company stores for factory workers in the North. In both cases, the labor force was exploited and often held hostage by the indebtedness that was either required or strongly encouraged by those economic systems. So, as I would approach African Americans to generate the larger sums of money that Impact needed to move forward, I was often left with little to show for my efforts.

Appearing at Campus Crusade for Christ fundraising events was of little encouragement. In the 1990s they were held under the auspices of History's Handful, CCC's strategy to identify one thousand people to commit 1 million dollars each toward the Great Commission. I would appear at these events to find myself in a sea of White Christians, most of whom were politically conservative Republicans, and find it difficult to gain their attention. They were usually hearing about a variety of ministries, and frankly, it was hard for Impact to compete. On the one hand, you would hear presentations about The JESUS Film Project, CCC's premier global evangelistic initiative led by Paul Eshelman and later by Jim Green. They had developed their strategies and worked out the numbers to demonstrate that for every dollar you gave, another soul would be saved somewhere around the world. On the other hand, there was the array of ministries targeting inner-city youth, from Here's Life Inner City to Student Venture, Campus Crusade's high school ministry. Our core audience was African-American college students. For most people, our target represents those African Americans that are of the least concern. College students are perceived as on their way to making it. When donors think about the needs of the African-American community, they think of the permanent underclass or others who are in desperate need. Most fail to recognize the strategic significance of a dynamic, vibrant, Christ-centered, and culturally relevant ministry to this pivotal audience, African-American college students.

A significant moment occurred in the spring of 1996 when I was invited to attend yet another History's Handful event in

Daytona Beach. I had learned a few years before that it was best to bring Rebecca to these occasions, because my wife is much more gregarious and winsome than I am and because most of those who attend these events do so as couples. But, I went ahead and recall vividly the heated conversation I had with God on the sixty-minute drive there. I contended that I was wasting my time, complained about the discomfort I felt being there, and asked Him why in the world He had me going to that event. My initial exposure to the event did nothing to allay my concerns. Bill McCartney, founder of Promise Keepers, was one of the featured speakers, but his message of reconciliation seemed to be at cross-purposes to our mission and calling.

I had to go back to get Rebecca for the second day of the event, and after ensuring that our children were in good hands, we arrived at the conference just in time for lunch. Jim Topmiller, the director of fund development of the campus ministry, had set up a fifteen-minute meeting during the lunch hour with Jim and Jane Corman and Chuck Dettling, who oversee the Corman Foundation. They began to ask questions that surprised Rebecca and me, revealing that they had been thinking about the challenges of ministry to the Black community on a deeper level than most. They continued to ask questions even after our original fifteen-minute allotment had expired, asking several other major ministry leaders if they could wait or reschedule. In the end, they committed an incredibly generous sum to us for the year and began giving on an annual basis. They not only gave to our proposals but suggested and offered to fund an internship program to get recent graduates to serve with us for one or two years in order to breathe new life into our still-stagnant recruiting efforts.

This represented a sea change in the fortunes of our fledgling effort. Impact '96 saw 1,850 students attend, and in my closing challenge I called for people to commit themselves to Impact, not just as a conference but as a movement. We introduced a document, The Impact Movement Commitment, and asked conferees to sign it as an expression of their commitment to living out this vision throughout the course of their lives. The idea of The Impact Movement was born.

RYAN'S STORY

At the Impact Conference on December 28, 1996, I learned of Jesus' love for me and accepted His invitation to be my Savior. My Heavenly Father, I also learned, had created me *intentionally*, with a purpose and plan that only I could fulfill.

I had intended to attend law school after graduation. Instead, I served as an Impact intern on my college campus following graduation. My responsibility was to strategically engage students, many of whom had come to know me in my earlier days as anything but a Christian, in discussions about God.

I reached out to the college's Black student organizations, my former football teammates, and anyone else who would listen. I led Bible studies, hosted all-campus lectures and led a group of students on a mission trip to Zambia, Africa.

Following my internship, I enrolled in law school and am now a civil rights attorney. My wife, Charity, and I also co-lead 40 teenagers from our neighborhood in Newark, where only four out of 10 students graduate from high school. I implement many of the tools I learned as an Impact intern.

It's hard for me to comprehend how drastically my life changed after meeting my Father, my heavenly Father, at Impact '96. And I am anxious to see where my relationship with Christ continues to take me.

—RYAN PAUL HAYGOOD
CO-DIRECTOR, POLITICAL PARTICIPATION GROUP
NAACP LEGAL DEFENSE & EDUCATIONAL FUND, INC.

Impact '98 continued our growth trajectory, as 2,450 people gathered in Atlanta. We wrestled with how to best steward the momentum and enthusiasm of the students and alumni. Our efforts to get the structures and systems of Campus Crusade for Christ to respond to this movement were frustrating. This was not because of any ill will or reluctance to engage the challenge on the part of our coworkers in Crusade, but we always found ourselves trying to figure out how to retrofit CCC systems and strategies to serve the constituents of The Impact Movement. Great trial and error occurred, with the encouragement of Steve Sellers to "do what it takes" to see the movement grow and for more and more African American students to be reached.

Nevertheless, there were some significant chafing points. One had to do with the high degree of specialization of ministries and the specificity of mission that existed within Campus Crusade. While we were a part of the campus ministry of CCC, our conferences typically had a twenty percent post-college and ten percent high school student attendance. This was because our alumni would often return to their churches and volunteer to lead youth ministry. They wanted their most advanced high school students to have the exposure of the Impact conference to give them a vision for what their college experience could be like. Our vision, from the outset, was to reach our community as well as the world, while the CCC motto had always been "The campus for Christ today, the world for Christ tomorrow." Skipping over the community just does not fly with Black students and young professionals.

Internationally, we discovered in 1995 that the Worldwide Student Network had stopped sending teams to sub-Saharan Africa. This was due to the unpredictability of the calendar of the universities, the political instability of many of the countries, as well as some backlash against White western missionaries in that part of the world. So Kevin Werst approached Bobby

Herron, long-term staff member with CCC's Athletes in Action ministry, about leading an effort to take teams to Africa under Impact's auspices. He did so for many years, and to date we are the largest sender of African Americans as missionaries (mostly short-term) to the continent. That reality was greatly aided by what occurred at Impact 2000.

We invited Bekele Shanko, Campus Crusade for Christ's director of affairs for southern and eastern Africa, to be our international speaker for Impact 2000. In his impassioned message, he spoke of the miraculous power of God as manifested in his father's life, who received the ability to read the Bible despite never being taught to read in any language. He shared his vision, called Operation Sunrise, to reach fifty million people in fifty cities during a fifty-day period in 2002, and he asked all of us to join him. We geared up to do so, and partnering with many of our Campus Crusade for Christ friends, that summer we took more than three hundred people, nearly all of which were African American, to southern and eastern Africa. That is the single largest mobilization of African Americans for a missionary effort in history. Bekele also challenged our students to give, not to his ministry but to support The Impact Movement. He believed that the bulk of the funding for Operation Sunrise would come from Africa, and he challenged us to believe God for the bulk of our funding to come from our own community as well.

OPERATION SUNRISE AFRICA

When Bekele Shanko, director of affairs for southern and eastern Africa for Campus Crusade for Christ, spoke at the national Impact conference in 2000, he challenged The Impact Movement to join him in his vision to see 50 million people reached in a 50-day period in 2002 by targeting 50 cities in Africa. The result of that invitation yielded approximately 300 African Americans who said yes by heading over to participate on a short-term mission trip during the summer of 2002. The Impact Movement's mobilization of African Americans in missions during Operation Sunrise Africa is the largest effort of its kind in history. The results of the campaign, of which we were a small part, were phenomenal. Three hundred Christian organizations and 20,000 church congregations participated in exposing more than 64,000,000 people to the gospel. More than a million indicated their decision to receive Christ.

Odori Pendleton was one of those who participated in Operation Sunrise. "It built me up as a leader," says Odori of her involvement in Operation Sunrise. She cites learning more about the responsibility of a leader in relation to good stewardship of God's Word and being completely satisfied through sharing God's Word on the campus of the University of the Western Cape, among the things she learned there. Today Odori is a teacher in Northern Virginia, influencing the next generation of leaders for Christ.

At Impact 2002 we celebrated that achievement but actually experienced a continuation of a trend that first manifested itself in 2000. Our attendance numbers were slightly lower than they had been before. I sought counsel, prayed, and wrestled with that reality. I concluded in 2001 that Impact was losing steam due to the difficulty of attempting to manage and fuel the movement through the structures and systems of Campus Crusade for Christ. Steve Sellers's encouragement to "do whatever it takes" continued to echo in my mind. Rebecca and I began to have a series of casual conversations with Steve Douglass, first in his role as executive vice president of Campus Crusade for Christ and then as the president-designate, about what it would take to see a vibrant, vital movement be sustained and grow in the African-American community. The conversation was, in essence, an attempt to answer the question, How much separation is enough? For me, the answer had always been "as little as possible." I had no desire to reproduce the infrastructure, systems, and policies that Campus Crusade had developed over its fifty-plus years of existence. Nor did I want to do anything that seemed counter to the biblical mandate for unity within the body of Christ. Yet, Campus Crusade for Christ's systems and structures at times did not serve Impact well. They were fine structures for Campus Crusade for Christ, but they had not evolved with Impact in mind, and to alter them to make them responsive to Impact seemed to cause more harm than benefit. As Campus Crusade continued to reorganize and explore ways of doing ministry in the wake of Dr. Bill Bright's[1] passing, these questions became more acute, so much so that we were invited to a meeting of the U.S. leadership of Campus Crusade for Christ to present the case for Impact.

God brought together an outstanding team to make the case. Jim Hill, a public relations consultant who had cut his teeth as an executive at Burrell Communications, which had pioneered marketing to African-American audiences, joined Jacqueline Bland, Thomas Fritz, Rebecca, and me in explaining much of the reality and the strategy of The Impact Movement. We four CCC staff had a combination of over one hundred years of ministry as a part of the organization. The results of the meeting were inconclusive, but the process served to clarify the challenge it would be for The Impact Movement to become what it needed to be as a part of the Campus Crusade for Christ structure.

Thomas, Rebecca, Jim Williamson, and I began to meet to talk about the opportunity to craft the new structure of The

Impact Movement. Jacqueline signed on to lead the field component of our ministry, and Anthony Johnson agreed to lead our fund development effort. Melody Gardner moved to Orlando to help with the campus ministry as well. At the same time, I approached Steve Sellers about our desire to strike out as an independent 501(c)3. He urged us to consider being a subsidiary, but my sense was that being in that posture would put us at a disadvantage with many African-American and other donors who were willing to give to Impact but not if it remained a part of Campus Crusade for Christ.

These conversations were possible because of the heart, passion, and humility of Steve Sellers. Throughout my time of service with him, he demonstrated in a variety of ways his sense of brokenness over the history of race relations in this country and in the church. At the national staff conference in Colorado in 1995, he and I led the Campus Crusade staff in a prayer based on Daniel 9, confessing the history of racism in the church and asking God to deliver us from the consequences of the sins of previous generations. Dr. Bright responded to that time in tears, calling for the creation of a fund to help level the playing field so that more Black individuals would join the staff of Campus Crusade for Christ. Craig Fuhrmann proposed the idea of inviting Campus Crusade staff to designate one percent of the support they raise to supply this fund. This proposal was implemented in 1997 and continues to this day as the Ethnic Minority Assistance Fund. Yet, Steve was willing to acknowledge that, despite all of these positive steps, we were not seeing the growth that we all desired to see.

With Steve Sellers's sponsorship, we took our plan to Steve Douglass, who was by that time president of Campus Crusade for Christ. Steve Douglass has demonstrated a remarkable willingness to think beyond simple organizational viability and preservation. I admire the man greatly and have sensed God's hand on him in a special way since the day he was announced as successor to Bill Bright. After explaining our plan, he agreed to help us launch Impact as its own organization. He offered the systems and services of Campus Crusade for Christ to aid us in that process. In response to the generous, kingdom-minded spirit of these conversations, and in light of the vision and faith of Bill Bright, the inaugural board of directors of The Impact Movement ratified a covenant partner resolution, declaring our commitment to working together with Campus Crusade for Christ wherever it would advance the kingdom.

The final operational step came in the wake of these conversations. Several of us had prayed and fasted for direction in the fall of 2003. In December, The Impact Movement leadership team held a planning retreat, at which we mapped out where significant Impact works were located and where our staff and fellows (one- to two-year post-baccalaureate interns) were placed. We discovered an alarming fact. There was an inverse correlation between where our staff members were located and where our strongest local chapters had developed. We also assessed the fact that our staff were discouraged, isolated, and feeling unfruitful. Many were considering moving on to other things. As we considered these facts and the operational challenges of launching a new organization, a plan emerged. We would invite our staff and fellows to come to Orlando, participate in developing the new infrastructure, and resource our local campuses using a distance-coaching model.

The more we talked, the more enthusiastic we became. We decided to describe our local ministries as Impact chapters, which Black students relate to readily in light of the Black Greek system (that is to say, national sororities and fraternities). We also concluded that asking students to lead has great power. One of the realities that we observe is that Black students with leadership gifts are sought after by a number of campus organizations. A traditional Campus Crusade campus ministry-staffed approach, which typically results in a student needing to be involved for at least a year before being entrusted with leadership responsibility, means that these Black student leaders are often already in a leadership role in one or more other organizations by the time they are considered for leadership in ministry. Even if a staff member serving locally wants to accelerate and open up the leadership approval process, they must still overcome the fact that quite often in the Black community, ministry is viewed as the job of the "minister." Our staff members are typically perceived as campus ministers, and so the students often do not perceive themselves as responsible for the ministry. We discerned that by entrusting students to lead our local chapters, ownership, responsibility, and commitment would increase, leading to more effective local works.

Our plan was to take this proposal to the Ethnic Student Ministry regional directors,[2] who were responsible for the Impact staff in their various regions. It involved implementing this strategy over the course of a year, having those staff who agreed to come to Orlando make the transition during the summer of 2005. The regional directors' response was, "If this is the right thing to do, why wait?" After some discussion, we planned to implement the transition in the summer of 2004. At the same time, Dirke and Lorna Johnson agreed to join our effort; Dirke as director of human resources and Lorna as a part of our field coaching strategy. We held an Impact staff conference in Charlotte, North Carolina, in April 2004, explaining our case and inviting the staff to join us in Orlando. To our great delight, over 90 percent agreed to relocate in order to participate in this grand experiment. The Impact Movement, Inc., was on the map.

MELODY'S STORY

"Oh, God, I don't know what You are going to do, but You have got to do something!"

These were the desperate words I cried out to the Lord one evening in 1985 after attending the weekly meeting of a campus ministry my freshmen year at UNC-Chapel Hill. I grew up worshiping in a small Black church—and I was a minority in my secular world—so I wanted so much to connect more with African Americans. And see them connect with the Lord. I could not believe it: in a room of 200-plus Caucasian students, there were only three African Americans. My heart grieved continuously that ethnic groups were not being exposed to the person of Christ and eternally influenced.

Nearly two decades later, in the spring of 2003, I received a call from the president of The Impact Movement challenging me to move to Orlando, Fla., and join a team who would launch The Impact Movement, Inc. The Lord brought back to my remembrance the scene back on my high-rise balcony when I cried out for Him to do something.

God *has* done something; something amazing!

No longer do I worry that African American college students do not have an opportunity to encounter Christ in a way that is relevant to them. Through Impact, God has rescued thousands of African American students from the kingdom of darkness and saved thousands more from a Christian life filled with compromise and regrets.

I think of Quiana, who was far from the Lord and angry when she first encountered Impact. Today she is an infectious Christian who shares the Lord with every one around her. She did a fellowship with Impact, came on staff, and went on to seminary to pursue a degree in counseling to help reach "the least of these." Quiana is one of many. He put the prayer in my mouth back in 1985 and then, like only God could do, He chose to send me to answer this prayer.

—MELODY GARDNER
IMPACT STAFF MEMBER

ANTHONY'S STORY

Growing up in Woodbridge, Virginia, church was admittedly one of several "forced fun" activities. One Sunday in the fall of 1976, when I was 10 years old, I decided to really listen to the message. It was the first time in my life that I clearly understood the gospel, realizing there were indeed consequences for my choices. I vividly remember walking down the center aisle toward the front of the church with at least 100 eyes glued to my every step. A deacon joined me and showed me how to begin a personal relationship with Christ.

I didn't understand it, nor could I describe my inexplicable joy. While my faith was established and continued throughout my teen years, the spiritual dimension of my life exploded after I graduated from college and worked in corporate America; no doubt due to necessity. I got involved in Campus Crusade's ministry to professionals, Priority Associates. I also began to understand God wanted to control every aspect of my life, including my career.

Less than two years later a friend challenged me to consider attending a conference called Impact '91. Since I worked as an assistant buyer for a major Washington, DC, retailer, I was convinced I would not get the holiday time off to attend the conference. To my great surprise, my boss granted me the time off. And to confirm her decision, my landlord, more affectionately known as Deacon Wingfield, suggested I forego my rent to pay for the conference. As a strong believer, he sensed the Lord was up to something. It was true serendipity.

At the conference, a speaker gave a challenge and said, "If God asks you to go anywhere in the world to serve Him, and you would go, stand up." The more I thought about his question, the more convinced I became that I would go if called. I began to wonder, *Is He possibly calling me to the mission field?* I looked to my right and left, and realized I was in fact one of many standing. Never had God spoken so clearly to me as He did at Impact '91.

When I returned home and told my landlord I was going to become a missionary, he said, "I knew God had something for you there." He also said he didn't want me paying rent or buying groceries while I raised support to join Priority Associates in 1992. In fact, he chose to pay the remaining balance on my car note, which lasted another year. That gentleman became my very first supporter at $100 per month.

After a few years of serving with Priority Associates, Charles Gilmer called a meeting of people who had been affiliated with Impact. He cast the vision for what Impact should become. Impact had made such an indelible impression on my life that the least I could do was help them raise money for that vision. I became the Impact fund development director and served in that role from 2000 to 2006.

I live to motivate and challenge people to become all they can be for the cause of Christ, while empowering them to become generous givers to His work. It is my life's work. That passion developed because I saw what a difference Impact made in my life and I thought, *Wow, this should be multiplied a thousand fold. If I can be a part of exponentially increasing the number of people who are affected, then I'd be remiss not to do that.*

—Anthony Johnson
Financial Advisor

7
WHY IS THIS NECESSARY?

"Can we all get along?"

—RODNEY KING, ATTEMPTING TO QUELL THE 1992
LOS ANGELES RIOTS PROMPTED BY HIS
POLICE BRUTALITY CASE

W HY DO WE have to have a distinct ministry to address young leaders of African descent? Up to this point, this work has provided an anecdotal answer to this question. In this chapter, we will consider the philosophical and theological basis for this approach.

As I write, it has been sixteen years since Rodney King's voiced the question printed above, yet the question, slightly modified into, Why can't we all get along? is still voiced by many today. Latent racial tensions threatened to percolate to the surface in the 2008 presidential race. Unfortunately, Black and White Christians too often find themselves on opposite sides of the public debate. The biblical mandate for unity in the body of Christ is unquestionable. Does that mean that ethnic-specific ministry is out of place? Should not our goal be to become a reconciled body of believers? What does that mean? What does that look like? It is important as we wrestle with these challenging questions to start by addressing the missiological challenge facing the Christian church in America. These are not new problems. As we will see, their roots run beyond the founding of this nation by its European colonizers. Moreover, how we engage the diversity of cultures that exist in the U.S. will shape what we embrace and celebrate as effective ministry.

THE SIGNIFICANCE OF CULTURE

Culture is a body of behaviors, attitudes, thought patterns, and practices that are shared by a particular group of people. Music, art, and literature are expressions of culture but they are not the only expressions of culture. For our purposes, it is important that we understand that everyone has a culture or is a part of a culture. Americans of European descent tend not to think of themselves as having a particular culture. Yet they do. It is what is commonly referred to as "White," and it's different from mine as a Black man. Those who see me function within a White context like Campus Crusade for Christ or at my child's predominantly White school may not realize that about me or other African Americans, because we have, for a variety of reasons, learned how to function in White culture. Therefore, we shift into White culture mode when we are operating in those environments. However, there are things about that mode of operation that are not my culture; they are not the way I grew up and not the ways I learned to relate—nor is it the environment where the origins of my Christian experience lie.

Another term that is helpful to understand is *contextualization*. Contextualization is a missiological term for taking the gospel and expressing it within the context of a particular culture. It describes an approach that clarifies the goal of evangelism and discipleship for a cross-cultural mission or missionary. It involves going beyond simple translations from one culture to another, such as translating a hymn from English to Spanish. It seeks to see expressions of Christianity develop that are culturally relevant or authentic, thereby entering the world or culture of that people group. It is an application of the incarnation of Jesus Christ to the cultural environments of the missionary endeavor. This is essential if the missionary wants everyone in that culture to hear and be exposed to a clear, relevant presentation of the gospel. When most modern missions operate overseas, contextualization is one of the unspoken goals. The implied objective is to see the ministry manned by nationals in a country. When we missionaries are pioneering ministry in another country, English speakers are often the initial target. The ministry reaches a different state of maturity when you have leaders who are able to minister with fluency in the language of that particular culture. That is a step in the process of contextualization.

The alternative is for a missionary or minister to conduct himself or herself in such a way that asks those of another culture to leave or diminish their culture in order to be discipled or recognized as legitimate Christian leaders. This has been the tendency of missionary efforts for millennia, dating all the way back to the Book of Acts. That was part of the drama that culminated in the debate in the Council at Jerusalem, described in Acts 15. Yes, the controversy was religious and theological in nature, about Jew and Gentile, but it was also about the Jewish culture being exported as part of the gospel. The decision of the council at Jerusalem, which God obviously sanctioned, was that "we should not make it difficult for the Gentiles who are turning to God" (Acts 15:19). They chose to remove Jewish expectations of what it meant to follow God from what was required to be a disciple of Christ. They stuck to the simplicity of the gospel.

A LESSON FROM HISTORY

The critical importance of contextualization to the missionary effort is illustrated by missiologist Ralph Winter. In his publication, *Mission Frontiers,* Winter reflects on the history of missions to the Native American populations: "Of the hundreds of tribal societies, not a single example exists of a truly indigenous, virile church movement."[1] It's not because there were never missions to the Native Americans, nor is it because Native Americans did not respond to the gospel. Hundreds of thousands of Native Americans became Christians. The reason there is not a significant Native American church today is that the missionary efforts that were conducted assumed that in order for a Native American to become a Christian, he or she had to become "White." Missionaries to the Native Americans often discussed the question, How do we make good "White men" out of these "savage Indians"? And so, when a Native American responded to the gospel, they were systematically pressured to abandon every vestige of their cultural identification and become culturally White. As a result, the White evangelical church consigned those who were resistant to leaving their culture to an existence without a culturally relevant expression of the gospel. No doubt, the latter reality has greatly contributed to the deplorable social situation we have today on many reservations.

A final note about contextualization: there are various versions of it. We advocate and practice what is sometimes referred to by missiologists as "critical contextualization," which requires that cultural adaptations and expressions of the gospel or responses to the gospel always be filtered through and limited by the mandates of Scripture. Some have accused us of watering down the gospel or of placing culture on equal footing with Scripture. That is not at all the case. That would be syncretism. Syncretism is that cultural-religious practice in which Christian forms and symbols are mixed with non-Christian religious concepts and forms of worship. This often results in extreme perversions of the gospel, reflecting a non-critical or more theologically liberal contextualization, which we reject. What we are doing in developing The Impact Movement is applying the same principle of contextualization to ministry in this country as has been applied internationally. Our goal is to speak the language, if you will, of those in the African-American community that White-led missionary efforts will not connect with otherwise. We are not willing to limit ourselves to being only with those who can speak the "White Christian" language or have assimilated into White culture. We are serious about raising up leadership that will develop ministry that is culturally relevant.

THE FOCUS OF IMPACT

The focus of The Impact Movement is reaching those of African descent on our campuses, in our communities, and around the world; but more specifically, it is reaching the person who would not be reached or discipled by mainstream ministries. When we talk about our target audience, we acknowledge that not all of us of African descent are alike. Our cultures have many different values, priorities, tendencies, and sensitivities. Within the family of cultures of African descent, there is a great deal of diversity. There are urban and suburban differences, northern and southern differences within those audiences. Some are from the Caribbean; some speak a variety of languages and dialects. Add to these variables generational issues. Particularly among recent African emigrants and those from the Caribbean, there are differences between first, second, third, and fourth genera-tions in each of these cultures.

THE ABCs OF ETHNICITY

Generally speaking, you can divide any ethnic minority group in this country into three categories. Keith Young, an Asian-American former colleague, and Jacqueline Bland developed a simple description of American ethnicity that we call "the ABCs of ethnicity." The *A* category is composed of those who have been assimilated into mainstream American society. This type of person may not have been raised culturally Black. They just happen to be of that heritage or background. They may have been brought up in the suburbs, gone to an all-White high school, lived in all-White neighborhoods, gone to all-White churches, and don't have any real exposure to their cultural heritage. As a result, they identify with the dominant culture. For others in this category, they may have grown up with some connections to the Black community, but they have chosen to immerse themselves in a White environment. This could be for any number of reasons. Perhaps it is the environment in which they came to know Christ and therefore they associate that experience, or being in that environment, with their Christian growth. It could be a practical decision, just to "go along to get along." In this case, the person perceives that White folk are in control, so they conclude, "I'm going be like them, so that I can enjoy the benefits they have." Sometimes a person chooses to assimilate out of a self-hatred or self-loathing that can be the product of being a minority in a society such as this.

The second type is the *B* category, which represents bicultural ethnic persons. The *B* person probably grew up in an ethnic community but was raised or learned to relate in the dominant culture. They can shift between the two cultures with relative ease and fluency in both. Groups like Campus Crusade have tended to engage a number of people like this in the course of doing ministry. Bicultural students may show up and hang around as long as they are being developed, resourced, or loved. However, they will tend to disappear when their cultural connections are jeopardized, when asked to make decisions that will hinder their ability to remain engaged in their own community, or when they feel their involvement or leadership is being limited or controlled. If they feel like they are being told what to do or made to do things in a "White way" or to adapt to White culture, they will disappear. Many of our White missionary friends have had experiences with this phenomenon over the years. I have had many conversations with CCC staff who describe working with a Black student for a while and then find themselves asking, "Where'd she go?" This student no longer connects with the ministry, has stopped showing up for meetings and appointments. The staff person later discovers that the student is now the president of the gospel choir or has started another ministry. These students are cordial, perhaps even friendly, but they do not really relate to CCC on an ongoing basis anymore. This is a common phenomenon with White para-church groups reaching out to ethnic Americans.

The last category completing our ABCs is that of the *C* ethnics. A *C* ethnic person is someone who is culturally or ethnically cloistered or, for want of a better term, contextualized. This person lacks the desire or perhaps the ability to function outside of their culture of origin. Very few White missionaries know anyone in this category. This type of person is not going to connect with White missionaries because they avoid White people in general. They will not respond to typical Campus Crusade or other para-church ministry initiatives. Either this person doesn't relate to what White Christian workers are saying because they speak a different "language," or they are not interested in what those workers are saying. So, they just don't show up on the radar screen of most White campus ministries and other types of para-church organizations.

Just because we are calling it the ABCs does not mean that *A* Black people are better than *B* Black people, who are better than *C* Black people. I know for some of my readers that will be your default assumption. This is not a grading system. It merely helps to keep our target audience in focus.

The Impact Movement's mandate is not to engage or reach assimilated African Americans. Campus Crusade for Christ and other groups do not need Impact to accomplish that objective. Assimilated African Americans are going to be reached by the programs that are executed to reach a general American audience. The Impact Movement exists to reach bicultural (B) African Americans and contextualized (C) African Americans. We in The Impact Movement are happy that God is calling assimilated African Americans to participate in the Great Commission with whatever organization and in whatever capacity that may be. That is a good thing. We are not trying to force people from this background to come join us. Assimilated Black folk are not who we exist to serve or to mobilize.

A word of caution to my White brothers and sisters: do not mistake the presence of an A person in your ministry as positioning you to get to B and C African Americans. Assimilated folks feel fine in the mainstream, and they may resent the effort to identify them with or task them to reach their culture of origin. Marketing research has revealed that most African Americans are most attracted to presentations in which fifty percent or more of the images are African-American.[2] This confirms that predominantly Black ministries are the kind of environments in which we bicultural or contextualized African Americans are most comfortable. That is when we feel most connected to that ministry. These same studies indicate that White people generally do not mind ads in which 50 percent of the models or actors are Black. However, those who are trying to develop multiethnic ministries are still confronted with a problem. If you are trying to create an image in which half of what you see is African American, how do you include other ethnicities and maintain a high enough presence of White people to make Whites feel welcome? I hope you catch the point. Trying to create venues that maintain momentum for ministry for a variety of ethnic identities is very difficult. Our desire is to generate venues that accelerate the momentum of ministry, not undermine it.

An implication of this analysis is that many of the complaints about White churches and White ministries not being diverse is misapplied criticism. C. Peter Wagner came under fire by many in the Christian racial reconciliation movement for his promotion of a "homogenous church growth" principle in church planting and church growth. He was missiologically correct. People cite Dr. Martin Luther King, Jr.'s frequent comment during the Civil Rights Movement that "the most segregated hour of Christian America is eleven o'clock on Sunday morning,"[3] and posit that it is still true. Segregation is the systematic exclusion of one or more groups from another group. According to that standard definition, our churches are no longer segregated. It is exceedingly rare (though regrettably not unheard of) in 2009 for a White church to ask a Black person to leave their worship or other services. I have never heard of a White person being asked to leave a Black church, even before the laws of the land prohibited segregation.

Frankly, from a missiological point of view, the Black church is an incredible missions success story. The Black church developed as the healthy, vibrant source of hope, help, and sustenance in the Black community that it is in part because the White church in this country, out of its prejudice, excluded Black people or treated us as second-class citizens of the kingdom of God. In so doing, they prompted Black Christians to create a space where Black leadership developed, Black hymnody emerged, and a powerful Black preaching tradition flourished. In other words, the White church in the eighteenth and nineteenth centuries did the right thing for the wrong reasons. Was racism in the White American church sin? Yes. But what men meant for evil, God meant for good. In God's providence, the independent Black church has a legacy that stands as a stark contrast to the history of missions to the Native American population in this country.

White churches and White ministries need to continue to maximize their effectiveness at reaching as many people as possible. If their ministry is effectively contextualized to reach White people, that is not wrong. May they reach even more people. If they in their missionary mandate want to work to foster ministries to other ethnicities, praise God for that. However, to assume that the path to ministry effectiveness with those audiences is to simply colorize their literature, their staff, or other aspects of their ministry is ultimately inadequate— even if well intentioned.

In the present day, there seems to be a notable interest in creating multi-ethnic churches or multi-ethnic ministries. I have no doubt that God is calling some to this endeavor and that there is a growing percentage of people in our country who are ready and willing to respond to that context of ministry. These individuals may have grown up in a multi-ethnic experience or have entered into a cross-cultural marriage. However, this is not an either/or but a both/and proposition. We need places of worship where those who are in that position feel comfortable and can encounter God in the context of a multi-ethnic experience. However, assertions that these sorts of ministries are God's ultimate design and therefore God's best assert too much.

First Corinthians 9:22, in which the apostle Paul states, "I have become all things to all men so that by all possible means I might save some," adds to my argument. It is not possible to be all things to all people *at the same time*. I cannot speak Spanish and English simultaneously. You cannot sing a Negro spiritual and White Contemporary Christian music in the same measure. The biblical counterbalance to the mandate of the aforementioned scriptures for ethnically or culturally focused ministry is laid out for us in 1 Corinthians 12. We are all one body, and it is wrong for us to assert that we do not need one another. However, the reality is that, when bringing people from disparate cultures together, one of two things is likely to take place.

Either one group's culture will dominate, forcing those from other cultures to adapt or conform, or the collective group will create its own "third culture," forcing everyone to adapt. This is problematic if the goal is to reach those who do not belong to anyone's church. We are, in this case, adding difficulties to those who want to turn to God, a violation of the principle of Acts 15:19. We need to celebrate the examples of effective multi-ethnic ministry that God is raising up, but we also need to celebrate the examples of effective ethnic-specific ministry that God is using to reach many for His kingdom.

Biblically, we must reexamine the passages in the Book of Revelation that many use to promote multi-ethnic ministry. The text says in Revelation 7:9, "After this I looked and there before me was a great multitude that no one could count, from every nation, tribe, people and language, standing before the throne and in front of the Lamb." Several things are noteworthy in this short passage. First, the ethnic and cultural distinctiveness of those assembled is preserved. Secondly, the repetition represented in "nation, tribe, people, language" seems to suggest an emphasis on the richness and breadth of that multi-ethnic assembly. Indeed, it communicates a spirit of celebration of those differences, not an attempt to set them aside. Their diversity is part of what makes their witness compelling. The remarkable thing here is that God, in His sovereignty, is using the reassembly of the peoples of the world as a visible display of redemption from the curse pronounced at the tower of Babel in Genesis 11. Just as the process of cultural differentiation was set in motion at that time, so now those various reflections of that image have been ransomed by the blood of Christ and reassembled to do what they should have done back then—give praise and glory and honor to the One worthy of such.

In John 17:20–23 Jesus prays for our unity, that the world might know that the Father sent Him. However, unity that requires cultural homogeneity impresses none of our onlookers. The world's criticisms of us are quieted when God raises up Christians from disparate cultures and causes them to be devoted followers of His, living out the gospel in the context of their culture, and we then come together around our common faith, our profession of Jesus as the Messiah. On rare occasions when such a thing occurs, the world looks on in wonder.

The Impact Movement's goal is to reach people of African descent. While we operate and minister in that family of cultural idioms, we exclude no one who is attracted to that expression. We are deeply grateful that our national conferences are five to ten percent non-Black.

MUHAMMAD'S STORY

I grew up as a Sunni Muslim in Cleveland Heights, Ohio. The faith of my family gave me a legalistic worldview. As a result of an abusive father, I tried to drown my pain in alcohol, sometimes to the point of passing out. This started when I was a freshman at Cleveland State University. I also experienced great fits of rage and hatred.

In an effort to get right with God, I got baptized in church, but it was an outward response, not at the heart level. I didn't receive Christ until I started to read the Bible on my own. When I read the Bible it reached my heart and saved my soul.

At Cleveland State University, Impact Staff invited me to a Fall Retreat. It was the beginning of my understanding of the decision I made at church. For the first time I heard about missions. Also I heard about the Holy Spirit and who He is. I saw a lot of young African American Christians who wanted to live like I did. I thought, *This thing has purpose. It has meaning. It's not just something I go through or just feel emotionally. It's something I can live.*

In 2002, I heard Charles Gilmer paint a vivid picture of how we, as African Americans, are the richest black people in the world, and that we have a responsibility of giving back. I felt God was saying, *This is your responsibility, this is your charge.* The next year after I graduated, I worked as a fellow on campuses in the Cleveland area and realized my passion: to help men grow in their faith.

I then left ministry to work with mentoring non-profits. I remember sitting across from an elementary-aged boy and realizing how the lack of a father figure was going to play out in his life. His need for Jesus was more than his need for me. I told the boy about Him, and it was then that I knew I was called to reach African American males for Christ, many like me who did not have a loving father.

I returned to Impact, where I coach students to reach other college students and get involved in the needs in their communities. I grieve for the lack of qualified Black men who can father the fatherless, guide, and mentor younger men. My passion is to see students like I was become men who will lead.

—MUHAMMAD HAFEEZ
CAMPUS MINISTRY COACH
THE IMPACT MOVEMENT

ABOUT RACIAL UNITY

Racial unity within the body of Christ is part of the vision of The Impact Movement. Those of us who know Christ have to help lead the way. Racial harmony in the broader society is a desirable goal, but sinners sin, so I do not expect those who have yet to experience the saving power of the Holy Spirit to be able to stop sinning in matters of race. Rather, it is the members of the body of Christ who are called to be "salt and light" in our society. (See Matthew 5:13–16.) When the body properly serves that function, it does have a restraining and preservative effect on our society. When it fails to do so, it leaves a society open to great evil.

There is no more graphic illustration of this principle than the events that led up to the Civil War. Virtually all of the major denominations in the American church split North from South several years before the nation divided itself at the outbreak of the Civil War. As a result of the failure of the church to be "salt and light" in this area, we fought a war that cost more American lives than were lost in all our other wars combined.

In order to understand God's ideal in regards to reconciliation, let's take a look at the biblical texts that address this issue, explore what went wrong in Black-White relations in the American church, and why many Black Christians are not enthusiastic about racial reconciliation. The terms *reconciliation* or *reconciled* are found in the New Testament several times, most notably in 2 Corinthians 5:18–19 and Ephesians 2:11–21, and many build a theology of racial repair based on these and other such passages. However, a careful reading of these passages reveals that the word is not used in relation to men being reconciled one to another or group-to-group. The relationship that is referred to as being reconciled is always man's with God, not man's with man. Now, many passages teach that it is God's desire and intention that the body of Christ be one. (See John 17:20–23; 1 Corinthians 12; and Ephesians 4.) It also indicates that this is the actual spiritual reality, whether we acknowledge it or not. I have yet to find a passage where the unity that we all are called to manifest with our brothers and sisters within the body of Christ is referred to as a product of reconciliation.

Perhaps the place where the terms *reconciled* or *reconciliation* occur in the closest connection to teaching on relationships within the body of Christ occurs in Ephesians 2:16. The context of verses 11–21 is certainly addressing the relationship between Jews and Gentiles. The passage concludes its comments on that relationship, declaring that those who were formerly viewed as Jews and Gentiles are "one new man" in verse 15, and "one body" in verse 16. Verse 16 states, "And in this one body to reconcile both of them to God through the cross, by which he put to death their hostility." Yet, even in this context, the point of the phrase "to reconcile both" has to do with both Jews and Gentiles alike being reconciled to God, as one man. The clear point of this passage is that we all, both Jews and Gentiles alike, stand in the same desperate need and all have access to God's divine provision for that need, Jesus Christ.

As a Black Christian, this more careful reading of the biblical text raises several concerns and a crucial point of understanding. Let me start with the understanding. Why have people found it necessary to co-opt (and from our brief study, misapply) this most powerful term, *reconciliation*, to address racial issues in this country? I believe it is because the White church in this country had so long defended or acquiesced to the unbiblical practices of this nation during slavery and in the Jim Crow era that Christian activists were looking for the most powerful, compelling principle they could in order to break through the blindness, callousness, and biblical sophistry often employed to defend those racist practices. While I agree with much of the goal of that effort, we must be careful which principles and which texts we use to pursue those goals lest we tread on prerogatives that belong to God alone. In other words, if God's major concern is that we be reconciled to Him, when we mix or mingle our need for unity and justice with His claim on us for a right relationship with Him, we are in a treacherous place. God tolerates no rivals. If we think these "reconciliation" passages and that term are somehow the province of efforts to repair race relations, we are taking something that belongs to God and applying it in the wrong place. Clearly, biblical unity is important, and the unwillingness to live in obedience to clear biblical teaching concerning it is the essence of the historical sin of racism in the White American church. The Bible is very clear on these matters. We need not add more weight to the biblical mandate for Christian unity than it already possesses.

We Black Christians are, much to the surprise of many of my White Christian friends, very loyal to the Scriptures. This is why, as George Barna has observed through his polling, the Black American community as a whole is more committed to biblical social standards than the White community.[4] We take the Bible very seriously. So, these sorts of biblical misapplications cause a serious amount of difficulty in us.

Additionally, to hearken to the term *reconciliation* suggests that there was a time in the past when we were in some sort of harmonious relationship. Now, it is true that early converts to Christianity from the slave or free Black populations may have assumed that they would be treated with respect as "fellow-heirs of the grace of God" by their White Christian contemporaries. The sad reality is that this was not the case. This tragic failure led to the birth of the Black church, in order to create spaces where Black Christians could enjoy their relationship with God without the indignities and inconsistencies they experienced from their White brothers and sisters. As was discussed earlier, it was the right thing to do, but it happened for the wrong reasons. As a result of that history, I suppose one could argue that we are trying to return to a state of innocent enjoyment of the kind of unity that God originally intended. However, as a fourth generation (at least) African-American Christian, the idea of "returning" to the state of relationships my ancestors had with their White Christian peers is immediately repulsive—remember, my ancestors were slaves—and reveals on the part of my White brothers and sisters who approach me in that way an insensitivity that borders on a willful naiveté. In many cases, further conversation has revealed that in many instances their responses are indeed willful in their reluctance, and at times refusal, to engage sins that reach back that far. But, for African Americans, to do less is not really reconciliation. It smacks of a desire to return to the "happy times" to which so many Whites, particularly in the South, have voiced a desire to return. If that is what is in any way hinted at in a reconciliation context, we Black folk want no part of it!

Finally, there is a problem related to the analogy that is easily assumed from the scriptural context itself. The Ephesians 2 passage, with its primary teaching concerning Jews and Gentiles, has some potentially uncomfortable dynamics associated with it from the point of view of an African-American Christian. Most of us have no problem at all with the biblical text. However, when it is applied to Black-White relationships, the question always lingers in our minds, Who are you viewing as being in the place of the Jews and who is in the place of the Gentiles? Clearly, the Jews were in the more favored position spiritually. They are the people through whom the Scriptures and the Messiah had come to the world, so we Black Christians resent being placed in the Gentile position in that analogy. It suggests that the theology, songs, and practice of the Black church are substandard, or less worthy, and that Black Christian leaders are not the peers and equals of their White counterparts.

My White Christian colaborers frequently want to find a Black Christian with whom they can build a relationship in the name of "reconciliation." That is a good thing, a healthy step. However, it is merely one step in the long journey to wholeness that the

American church must engage if we ever want to overcome the generations of sinful attitudes and actions that characterize our collective history. Moreover, the church is in great peril of being rendered irrelevant by its relative slothfulness in this regard. Those who do not know Christ are often way ahead of Christian believers when it comes to developing racial sensitivity. The political process and its landscape are no help in this matter. The fact that most of my White Christian friends are Republicans and most of my Black Christian friends are Democrats is an obvious illustration to me that we have not gotten very far in this.

The Southern Baptist Church's declaration of repentance in 1995 was a very positive step, but it was only a step.[5] It possessed the previously mentioned flaw of refusing to take responsibility for the sins of previous generations, which we will discuss in the following call to prayer as the biblical prescription for how to respond when one confronts the consequences of a previous generation's sin. (See Leviticus 26:40–42.) As the news reports at the time indicated, Black church leaders were not, and are still not, sure how to respond to such actions and their attendant overtures, for often the invitation to enter a reconciled relationship involves an expectation that you will join—to become a part of—in the aforementioned instance, the Southern Baptist Convention, or some other organization, church, fellowship, etc. This is good from the perspective that we Christian organizations and institutions should always maintain an inclusive posture, especially in light of the fact that that it has not always been the reality. Yet the implicit devaluation of Black Christian entities, institutions, and their leaders that is communicated by such an expectation is problematic. The White "inviter" seems to assume that since they have more resources, larger numbers of participants, or a longer tradition of theological reflection, that Blacks should want to be a part of their organization. I suppose there is a natural impulse to want to see Blacks included in light of the history of exclusion, but we cannot go back to the moment when White churches decided to exclude or treat their Black converts or members as less than equals. That time has passed and, as was discussed earlier, a diverse family of vibrant, relevant, and spiritually potent Black Christian traditions have emerged.

The real opportunity in racial matters within the body of Christ is for us to choose to stand together, not apart from one another, in a world that is waiting for us to play our God-ordained role as salt and light. That type of unity is persuasive to those outside the ark of safety. We need to be much more concerned with our unity, for it is a reflection of Christ's image. Do White Christians respect the leadership of Black Christian leaders and their spiritual tradition, and that of cultures other than their own? Do my White counterparts see Black Christian leaders as peers, or as those who must learn their ways, adopt their views, and practice Christianity in the same way that they do? The body of Christ is intended to live out the truth that we are interdependent on one another. We have a long way to go to figure out what it means to live out 1 Corinthians 12 in the American church. Many of us are still functioning in a manner in which we are not sensitive to the realities of our brothers and sisters who are in need. Others are more allied with a political party or ideology than we are to the cause of Christ. Are we really concerned about Jesus' view of the things that take place in our society? We are still far from what God is calling us to be and do. We are not very salty, nor do we shed much light. Until we figure out what it means to relate to one another as peers and equals in the body of Christ across color lines, we will continue to struggle in our effect on society.

This is the rub with many of the racial reconciliation efforts to date. In many instances they do an inadequate job of addressing the power relationships within the body of Christ.

Some of the models of reconciliation that have gained a lot of attention involve White Christians going into the inner city and addressing needs there. Some seek to mobilize middle-class White Christians to move into the city and to "live out reconciliation" in a poor inner-city neighborhood. While I admire those who have done so and applaud the good work that they have accomplished, there are some problems with that approach. Even though you might produce a church that is racially mixed, there is seldom equality in power in that congregation. For some who were once middle-class suburbanites, sacrifice may mean giving up their vacation in Europe, while the people who are indigenous to that inner-city community may be happy to scrape together the money to visit their relatives in another city. There is not equality in the empowerment the two groups feel. Being together is good, but it may not produce true peer relationships. Creating true unity in this instance is extremely difficult because the power in those relationships is still unequal. What I am recommending is that we prioritize reaching people in the context of their culture, allowing leaders to develop in that context and then bringing people together from various cultures to pray, leader to leader and peer to peer.

The Great Commission Is Paramount

Therefore, in The Impact Movement, though we are committed to unity in the body of Christ, we are convinced that there must first be contextualized outreach and ministry development. Our outreach needs to ensure that we get the gospel to every person. Our concern is not that we achieve some form of Christian political correctness or feel good about how we relate to one another, particularly at the early stages of ministry. Biblical unity is not about coming together for a photo opportunity or to support one political candidate over another. Instead, the future we all desire can be achieved as God raises up leaders out of various ethnic communities that are growing and developing and maturing in their leadership. We believe that as we come together as peers and equals, true biblical unity can happen.

A CALL TO PRAYER

The best place to express our unity is in prayer. In light of the histories that all the different ethnic communities have experienced in this country, the problems that have existed in the body of Christ, the lack of connections, and the multi-generational dynamics that are involved in the sin of the church in matters of race, it is clear that we really need to start building a foundation of prayer. John Dawson makes this case compellingly in his book *Healing America's Wounds.* If we hope to give leadership that addresses the root issues of our racial problems, if we want to create a foundation that will allow healthy relationships to develop, it is going to involve coming together on our knees before our heavenly Father to pray.

Too often is 2 Chronicles 7:14 cited in calls to national prayer without addressing the thrust of that text. It says, "If my people, who are called by my name, will humble themselves and pray and seek my face and turn from their wicked ways, then will I hear from heaven and will forgive their sin and will heal their land." For one thing, the promise is that if God's people "will humble themselves…and turn from their wicked ways," God will "heal their land." It is not addressed at those who do not know the Lord. All too often, Christians want to point out all the evils of this nation and pray that God will heal the country of these wicked influences in our midst. The text says we are to repent of *our* sin—the people of God's sin. As believers, we are instructed to deal with our sin, not the sin of those who are not redeemed.

The promise to Solomon recorded here is simply a restatement of that which was originally declared in the Mosaic Law.

In Leviticus 26:40–42 the children of Israel were instructed how they were to respond whenever they discovered that they were dealing with the consequences of a previous generation's sin. They were to confess their sins and the sins of their fathers. This has been a hard message for my White American Christians brothers and sisters to hear. American individualism has infected the church, producing a rather insular view of piety and responsibility. I have often had those who have sat under my teaching on this point insist that we cannot confess the sins of another in clear violation of what the text in Leviticus is instructing God's people to do. The prayer recorded in Daniel 9 is a very clear instance of a man of God practicing the principle of Leviticus 26. We do well to follow his example.

As it relates to building unity, sometimes less is more. Taking incremental steps, such as prioritizing praying together for one another's ministry and in light of the ugly history between the races in this country, actually gives us a chance to build a healthier environment for things that need to happen in the next stage of development. I would encourage us to begin praying through John 17, 1 Corinthians 12, Leviticus 26:40–42, and Daniel 9. As we come together from diverse backgrounds and diverse ethnicities to pray these kinds of prayers, God will move.

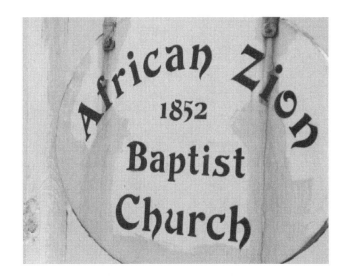

African Zion Baptist Church founded by ancestors of the author

Black Campus Crusade for Christ staff circa April 1987

Charles Gilmer, Emory Davis, Jr., Marcella Charles, and Tom Fritz at the African University Ministry Training Conference in Harare, Zimbabwe, 1986

Charles and Rebecca Gilmer during a lighter moment at Impact 2002

Conferees signing The Impact
Movement commitment form

A conferee committing to a bold
witness for Christ at Impact 2004

Thousands of students and marketplace professionals have gathered at
national Impact conferences over the years.

The Impact Movement's staff and fellows circa November 2007

The author's family, November 2008. From back to front: Charles, Rebecca, Karis, Caleb, Daniel, Jared, Micah, Joy, Chanel, Brittany, and Jamaica Gilmer

The annual Gilmer family photo (c. 1965). From back to front: Rev. Paul Gilmer Sr., Rodney, Paul Jr., Charles, Janet, mother Anna, and Vikki.

Charles Gilmer, age 17, 1977

Rev. and Mrs. Paul Gilmer and children at their fiftieth anniversary celebration,
August 1997

Rebecca and Charles Gilmer at their graduation from
the University of Pennsylvania, May 1981

First Baptist Church of Vandalia, Charleston, West Virginia, where the author grew
up and placed his trust in Christ (c. 1965). Charles Gilmer, third row, fifth from left.
Rev. Paul J. Gilmer, his father, was pastor.

8
THE IMPACT MOVEMENT, INC.

W HEN I ARRIVED at Cornell as a freshman, I knew no one on campus, except the host I had stayed with for the pre-freshman visit. I chose to live in the Ujamaa Residential College, a Black cultural studies living-learning program. Living in Ujamaa was a rich experience. I drank in the immersion in African-American culture that it provided.

The visiting lectures from men like Ron Karenga, inventor of Kwanzaa, were thought-provoking. I even got to hear Louis Farrakhan in one of his first public lectures after he reconstituted the Nation of Islam. I was struck with how well the man could *talk*. I knew he and I did not agree on the most important things in life, but his presentation was compelling, both mentally and emotionally. It was actually a rather chilling experience. Nine of ten points he would make were undeniably true and emotionally stirring, but about every tenth line he would say something that, if you bought it, would send you straight to hell.

The discussions in the dorm were a rich and varied stewpot of ideas. I relished the descriptions of city life offered by my classmates from New York City. I suppose half of the Black folk at Cornell were from one of the five boroughs, and their anecdotes began to give me increased confidence that I could handle myself in a large metropolis. To my surprise and pleasure, my display of Christian artifacts, my Christian commitment, and my Christian lifestyle did nothing to diminish my popularity.

I had no lack of mealtime conversations in the cafeteria, and some of my friends commented that my commitment to a girl in Philadelphia was limiting my options. I attended a local church with a number of other Black Christian students and attended a weekly Bible study led by a grad student who I met in Ujamaa. The recruiter in West Virginia had suggested that I look up Campus Crusade for Christ, but despite some periodic efforts to do so, I was never able to make contact. That was fine with me. I volunteered as a Big Brother through the church and was involved in organizing a Black Student Coalition on campus.

The Black Student Coalition effort became a clarifying experience. The people I worked with in that newly formed group disappointed me on several occasions. We planned a protest of South Africa's policy of apartheid during the inauguration of the president of the university. The pre-protest plan involved a silent, peaceful "walk out" with posters and placards to voice our position that the university should divest itself from the companies that did business with the apartheid regime in South Africa. As a freshman, I served as a marshal for the protesters. At the event, a couple of the upperclassmen went off plan and left shouting and trying to start a chant. It was very disruptive and not what we had discussed. The next time we had an opportunity to stage a protest, it was on the occasion of a board of trustees meeting. The plan was to stage a march and a sit-in, in order to get our grievances heard by the trustees. This time financial aid concerns were added to the apartheid agenda. The upperclassmen leaders agreed to march with representatives of NSCAR—the National Student Coalition Against Racism. When the march did not get the response desired, the NSCAR leader, a White student whom I had never met, began rallying the people to sit down in a wall across the entrance, lock arms, and blockade the building, trapping the board of trustees inside, until they acceded to hear our demands. Once again, this represented a total departure from the plan, and one that exposed our people to risks we had not evaluated and for which we had not prepared them. I left the rally in light of its hijacking by leaders whom I did not know or trust.

The personal inconsistency, immaturity, and instability of these leaders, combined with my ongoing study of the Bible, led me to a conclusion: social change was necessary, but if the people I had been working with were to be the leaders of a changed society, I had little reason to believe that our people would be any better off. The kind of change I was committed to required changed leaders as well as changed societal structures and practices.

How do you change people? Only one person in history claimed and displayed the power to do that, and His name is Jesus. I recognized the need to make winning people to Christ a priority in my agenda for social change.

Consider Jesus' discourse with some of the leaders of His day:

> To the Jews who had believed him, Jesus said, "If you hold to my teaching, you are really my disciples. Then you will know the truth, and the truth will set you free." They answered him, "We are Abraham's descendants and have never been slaves of anyone. How can you say that we shall be set free?" Jesus replied, "I tell you the truth, everyone who sins is a slave to sin. Now a slave has no permanent place in the family, but a son belongs to it forever. So if the Son sets you free, you will be free indeed."
>
> —JOHN 8:31–36

God has already planted the desire for such a movement in the hearts and minds of many of African descent here in the United States, in other parts of the diaspora, and on the continent of

Africa itself. As I have traveled this country for the past thirty years, casting this vision, I have run into people in whom God has stirred a desire to see the very things that I present come to pass. The Impact Movement envisions each community of African descent fulfilling its destiny as a reflection of the redemptive power of Jesus Christ. Those of us from the diaspora do not believe that our ancestors' suffering was a cosmic accident. We recognize that the slave trade that took our people away from the continent was not solely a result of European exploitation. There were Africans intimately involved in that trade, selling their kinsmen into a slavery unlike any known on the continent. I was asleep to this reality until a few years ago when Dr. Timothy Gyuse invited Rebecca and me to join him and his wife, Dr. Elizabeth Gyuse, for lunch. At the time, Dr. Gyuse, a Ghanaian, was the director of affairs for Campus Crusade for Christ's ministry in West Africa. Halfway through the meal, he said, "Betty and I wanted to have a meal with you, because God has been doing a work in our heart. In all of the talk of reconciliation, we want to be reconciled to our brothers and sisters in America. Our ancestors were involved in selling your ancestors into slavery. On their behalf, I want to apologize and ask for your forgiveness." I was a bit stunned. Forgiveness was quickly granted with tears and hugs. For me, this was a true process of reconciliation.

Yet, like Joseph's story in Genesis, what man meant for evil, God has used for good. Africans in America, despite our suffering and oppression, have prospered numerically and materially. There are some 38 million of us, and if we were our own nation, would be one of the largest economies on the planet.[1] We are the most prosperous Black people in the world. Could it be that there is a Joseph story waiting to be realized in us? There is no financial problem facing us for which we lack the resources, if we would use the resources that are passing through our hands in a responsible manner.

Our ancestors in the Western hemisphere were not the first Black Christians. Christianity in Africa is so ancient that it can rightly be described as an indigenous religion. The largest Christian church structures on the planet were in Africa through the fourth century A.D.[2] Those of us who have discovered this historical faith have found the gospel to be that which provides the best context to endure difficulties, clarify values, and provide the moral framework required to build a prosperous community. My own family heritage illustrates this. Most of the historically Black colleges and universities in America were founded in the church and continue to celebrate that religious heritage, sometimes with a loss of spiritual vitality but nonetheless with an undeniable debt to those who prayed and cried out to God in the name of Jesus in generations past. The NAACP, the Urban League, and virtually all the institutions and organizations that have worked to lift the state of our people have found their best refuge, their most generous investors, and their primary source of leadership in the Black church.

The worldwide church has been enriched by the contributions of its leaders of African descent. The examples abound, but from Martin Luther King Jr.'s leadership of this nation to live up to its claims of liberty and justice for all; to Desmond Tutu's calls for justice, then forgiveness and healing in South Africa; to the current leadership of Archbishop Peter Akinola of Nigeria in holding the line of biblical truth within the Anglican communion, the church has been blessed by those of African descent whose faith has fueled their leadership. Our spiritual songs and our preaching are still carrying the gospel to the nations. Even as this is written, the largest congregation in the increasingly spiritually cold United Kingdom and the largest church in continental Europe are both pastored by Nigerians.

When we, the children of slavery and colonialism, rise to prominence, God is glorified. God is seeking to birth a Joseph story as the children of the diaspora, whose ancestors were sold into slavery by their kin, return to the continent to add their expertise and resources to the restoration and redemption of the motherland. Africa is still writhing to shake off the lingering tendrils of colonial exploitation. If we unite, children of the continent and the children of the dispersion, we can perfect this process and allow Africa to experience the fruit of its vast riches, lay aside the sectarian and ethnic strife that cripples it, and raise up leaders who will steward their charge with the love and power of Christ. When God so moves, His ability to take pain and agony and bring out of it glory to Himself will illustrate His power to redeem the broken things of this world and give them health and fruitfulness. This is our vision.

OUR MISSION

The Impact Movement takes the truth of Jesus Christ to the campus, community, and world by producing leaders of African descent who are spiritually focused, financially responsible, and morally fit. This mission is extraordinarily significant for our community's health.

When we speak of being spiritually focused, we acknowledge that the spiritual heritage that is still so prominent in the Black community has lost a great deal of its edge. It has become a matter of culture not of conviction. We show up in large numbers on Easter and Mother's Day and neglect the other fifty Sundays of the year. Too many of us who do show up on the intervening Sundays are singing and shouting then, only to lay aside all Christian values, standards, and principles Monday through Saturday. It is time to stop being focused on the cares of this world and the deceitfulness of riches and to seek first His kingdom (Matt. 6:33). This means placing a priority on establishing and maintaining a vibrant relationship with God through Jesus Christ. Such a relationship is established by faith alone but is fueled by spending consistent time in God's Word and praying on a regular basis (Ps. 119:9–16; Phil. 4:6–7). We believe that we must live in a moment-by-moment dependence upon God's Spirit for daily living (Eph. 5:18; Gal 5:16–25). Our commitment is to seek to advance God's kingdom in everything we do and to be personally involved in obeying Christ's command to make disciples (Matt. 28:18–20; 1 Pet. 3:15). It is supported by involvement in a local church where the Bible is accurately taught and lived out (Rom. 12:4–8; Heb. 10:25). As we take part in that fellowship, we seek not to be served but to provide service (Matt. 20:28).

Financial responsibility means that we are to live out the biblical value of stewardship. This means that we affirm that whatever we have actually belongs to God. He has entrusted it to us for us to manage for His purposes. God owns it. We are to manage what God entrusts to us, including our money and possessions, as well as our time and talent. One of the manifestations of this is a commitment to live free of consumer debt. A believer trusts God to meet his or her needs. He is able to provide for our needs. We must discipline our wants in order to avoid such debt (Prov. 22:7). In order to do this we must plan our spending—being intentional and accounting for how we utilize God's resources (Luke 14:28–30). A variety of personal goals can be achieved if we rediscover the value of saving toward our short-term and long-term financial objectives (Prov. 6:6–8). Finally, all of this is to allow us to practice generosity. Those of us who are rich in the things of this present age are instructed to be generous and willing to share. God calls us to do good to all, especially to those of the household of faith. As stewards, we must invest our God-given resources in order to maximize our ability to fuel God's work (2 Cor. 9:7; 1 Tim. 6:17; Gal. 6:10).

We live in a day when many people think that biblically

defined moral fitness is an unrealistic objective. Yet, The Impact Movement calls on this generation to live by biblical standards as ordained by God and outlined in His Word. In light of the beauty of the truth that God has given us the gift of sexual desire, we commit to submitting our sexuality to the clear teaching of Scripture (1 Thess. 4:1–8). Abstinence until marriage is the only righteous, healthy, and socially responsible choice. While many want to focus on condom use as the means to "safe sex," study after study reveals that sexually transmitted diseases are on the rise and are found in the highest rates among Black people in this country. There is no other logical or reasonable approach to reversing these trends than to teach what the Bible teaches: abstinence from all forms of sex until marriage and faithfulness to one's spouse within marriage. Forgiveness and restoration are available to those who stumble along the way. Moreover, untold thousands have kept this standard. We must continue to call others to do so, as well.

We recognize that God is the Author of life and thus created us in His image. We will abstain from any form of violence or abuse (Gen. 1:27; 9:6). While there are multiple rationalizations for the violence and lawless acts that are all too common in our community, we must stop the cycle now. God desires truth in the innermost parts, and therefore we commit to living lives of integrity. We will not lie, cheat, or steal in ways subtle or explicit (Prov. 6:16–19).

OUR STRATEGY

Some have questioned our focus on college and university students. My recognition of the strategic nature of this population is very personal.

When I was a child, my love for reading led me to a rather curious habit. I would take books to church and read them during the service. As one of five children, the fact that I was quiet and not fidgeting during the service was probably enough to allow me to fly under the radar. My father's sermons were either over my head or covered highly familiar ground. I routinely tuned them out. It took a change in voice to wake me from my reading reveries.

On New Year's Eve of my sixth grade year (1970), my parents insisted that I accompany them to Watch Meeting. Watch Meeting is a service in which you "watch" in the New Year via a song and testimony service. This, of course, had little appeal to an eleven year old, who had plans of accompanying his cousins to the New Year's Eve roller-skating party at the local rink. After much protest, I grabbed my latest book and settled grumpily into the back seat of the car. Upon arrival at the church, I found myself a seat in the very last row of the church, far away from the eyes of the thirty or so people in attendance. The singing was what I expected, but as the evening progressed, one of the testimonies caught my ear. I laid my book aside and listened as a young woman from the church stood up and, in tears, described how her fellow students at West Virginia State College were harassing her because of her faith in Christ. She went on to talk about how Jesus was a comfort to her in this and that her faith was growing stronger through the ordeal. I was intrigued. I had never heard anyone under forty talk about having this kind of intimate communication with the Lord. I did not rush to the altar that night, but I did begin paying more attention in Sunday school and in church, asking questions both in my heart and of my teachers. This went on for several weeks, and, again, it took a change in routine for me to make the next step.

On Palm Sunday of the next year (April 4, 1971) my father came into Sunday school during devotions to explain to us the plan of salvation. He shared the same message that he delivered each Sunday toward the close of his sermon. We are all sinners in need of a Savior. Jesus is that Savior, the only begotten Son of God, sent to die on the cross to pay the penalty for our sin. All we have to do is receive Him as our personal Savior and Lord to be granted eternal life, escaping the torment of hell. Although I had heard this message hundreds of times before, hearing it in this setting allowed the truth to register in me. I rose from my seat and went forward, asking Christ into my life, along with seven other children my age. Most of us were boys. My father baptized all of us the following Easter Sunday morning.

I owe my salvation to the testimony of a college student. Students are the key to the future of communities of African descent. That they are the future leaders of our community is no shock to anyone. What may be a shock to some is the environment that college and university students enter when they enroll on campus. Virtually every campus has coed visitation, so sexual temptation is acute. Add to that the reality that in the U.S. the national ratio of Black female students to Black male students is roughly 2:1[3] (it is higher at many historically Black colleges and universities), and you have a scenario in which the women grow increasingly desperate of their marriage prospects and the men are tempted to exploit their intensified eligibility for their short-term gratification.

It is much more intense now than it was when I was a college student in the late 1970s. And it was bad then. Sexual promiscuity was tolerated, virtually assumed. Today, not to be sexually active is ridiculed in many settings on college campuses. This is true for both the men and women. The party buses pull up to campus before classes start in the fall, inviting freshman who are not yet old enough to buy a drink to attend parties off campus where drinking age laws are circumvented and the good times can roll. Dancing has devolved into clothed sexual pantomime, and the pressure to indulge is fierce. The distractions of twenty-four-hour cable, music pulsing through a device smaller than a credit card, and the party scene are an easy escape from the confusing and chaotic world created by the divergent ideologies and value systems being hawked on virtually every campus in the country. Egyptologists, "Christian" cults, and the occasional out-of-control fraternity or sorority threaten to capture the attention, time, and money of the unsuspecting student. Often, students who have been raised in the church and protected from much of this environment lose their way and flunk out of school, finding a way to remain in the neighborhood of their campus, pretending that they are still in good standing.

Many Black church leaders focus all their attention on getting their parishioners *to* college, failing to realize the dangerous gauntlet these unsuspecting but eager eighteen year olds are about to pass through. Too many of us adults look back on our college years with a wry amusement. We reflect on the mischief we participated in with a "boys will be boys" mentality and expect the next generation to do the same. We fail to understand that the temptations are more intense, the stakes are higher, and many a student is not making it through. We fail to appreciate the grace of God that kept us from the destruction with which we so cavalierly toyed.

The Impact Movement calls, equips, and supports both the men and the women involved in our movement to live according to biblical standards. The college age is also critical in that these students are establishing the patterns that will shape the rest of their lives. Our call to financial responsibility is key in this regard. As was noted earlier, our community is beset by a culture of indebtedness. We teach our students to break the cycle of debt, oftentimes countering the bad example and teaching of their families of origin.

We had a student a few years ago who, upon graduation,

wanted to join our staff. As a Christian non-profit, our pay structure is pretty modest. We ask for financial information from our applicants to help them determine whether they can afford to serve with us. In any case, those who join with us must trust God to provide ministry partners who will underwrite the cost of their participation in this mission. As we evaluated her application, we realized that, as a graduate of a private school, she had a hefty amount in school loans. We then discovered that on her graduation day her parents had declared, "You just graduated from college. You deserve a new car!" and drove to the local dealership. They then proceeded to walk her through purchasing a brand new, full-size car with no money down, offering nothing of their own to facilitate this purchase. That obligation, combined with her school loans, placed her in a financial position from which she could not afford to invest herself in full-time ministry. She could not sell the car for what she still owed on it. She had to get a job in the secular marketplace just to keep up with her loan payments.

Another phenomenon is that more students than you may realize are saddled with credit obligations and a poor credit history based on their parents having taken out credit cards in their name, maxing them out, and then failing to pay that obligation. We are entering into a partnership to help those in this position, but the point is, we must equip these emerging leaders with basic biblical principles of financial responsibility or we Black folk will continue to be dependent on others to address the financial problems in our community.

College students are a key in another respect as well. They are the foot soldiers who can begin to attack the persistent problems that are marginalizing portions of our community. College students possess the time, the technical or academic expertise, the cultural proximity, and the God-given passion to make a difference.

Bill Cosby, in his much-publicized remarks at Howard University in 2004, has said that the lower socioeconomic classes are not doing their part. I have a great deal of respect for his track record of philanthropy and developing television programming that delivers and supports positive values to and about our community. Nevertheless, while I appreciate the attention to the problem that his comments created, I disagree with the thrust of his conclusions. Those of us who have been blessed to take advantage of the opportunities this country affords are the ones who have failed. What do I mean by that? There is a great deal of rhetoric about "giving back" in our community. The problem is that at the point when an individual can make a meaningful difference—while in college and immediately thereafter—too many of our people are consumed with their own self-gratifying pursuits. My generation too often has said, "Let me get established in my career; then once I've got my legs under me, I'll give back." Fifteen years later, a marriage, two careers, three children, a house note, a car note, and probably too much debt render most powerless to give back in any meaningful way. If those graduates just raise their own children and are active members of their church, they have done better than most.

On college campuses, fraternities and sororities, which claim to be about serving, are much better known for their hazing, hard partying, and putting on a good step show. Our strategy in The Impact Movement is to get students involved in the community while they are in college. As we get college students involved in this kind of service, we are seeing them carry on this practice once they graduate. This is why we have had to build a high school component into our national conference program. Our alumni return to their churches, volunteer to lead youth ministry, and want to expose their high school students to "the Impact experience." Even if Impact college students only spend an hour a week helping a child learn how to read, as we grow this movement and multiply the number of those so serving, we can turn the notion on its head that doing well in school is a "White thing." I foresee a day when there are twenty thousand students involved in this movement, each taking an hour a week to invest in a child's ability to read.

College students have the discretionary time. They have the cultural proximity to relate to this hip-hop driven generation of young people. In addition, as college students, they are uniquely equipped to address the academic underachievement that is devastating our community. We need these students out there, whether Barack Obama is president or not. His achieving that office may have removed that glass ceiling and increased the hopes and aspirations of our children, but it will not automatically translate into the shoe leather required to address the real need—to read—that so many of our young people are not seeing met in their own lives. College students are critical to a campaign to change the fortunes of that portion of our community that is being left behind. Through these students we can do our part to lift them up to be able to see (and read) the American dream.

Our alumni do not want to be left out. In the spring of 2006, in the aftermath of Hurricane Katrina, we took nearly five hundred Black folk to New Orleans to help clean up the devastation. We were encouraged by the number of post-college adults who came to participate, taking their vacation time to join the students who were on their spring break. Our numbers were dwarfed by the Campus Crusade students, mostly White, who endured inadequate facilities and unhealthy work conditions to help bring the lower Ninth Ward back. They were in New Orleans because Rebecca, being a New Orleans native, used our network of relationships to identify pastors and others who could connect their parishioners who needed help with our Campus Crusade partners, Chip Scivique and Rick

Amos. FEMA told both Impact and Campus Crusade not to go there. There were thousands of FEMA-supplied beds in the neighboring 90 percent-White St. Bernard Parish. There were merely a few hundred in Orleans Parish, to which both Campus Crusade and we in Impact were denied access. But, The Impact Movement and Campus Crusade for Christ went anyway.

IMPACT NOW BY JUDY NELSON

When Hurricane Katrina hit New Orleans in 2005, the world watched in horror as the city's citizens cried from their rooftops for help, floated along it's historic streets amidst debris, and huddled against the storm seemingly abandoned by aid.

Impact's vice president, Rebecca Gilmer, was especially reeling. She grew up a cab driver's daughter, riding along with her father the streets that had become canals of heartbreak. She knew the churches who begged for help and longed to return the favors they had long granted her and her family. Since 1981, New Orleans' churches had sacrificially given and prayed for the Gilmers as one of their own had joined a mission field to raise up young African-American leaders for Christ.

Rebecca gathered two other women who then led the way for the Impact NOW (New Orleans Work) Project, the largest Black student recovery mission in New Orleans. With no money and little resources, Rebecca and her team began making contacts with the very churches who had long supported her ministry and now needed her support and prayers. Impact steered Campus Crusade for Christ's vast U.S. Campus Ministry network (USCM) to the places of greatest need.

"Impact leaders connected with local African-American leaders, organizations, and churches, then figured out how and where Impact and USCM students could best help," says Chip Scivicque, of the USCM. "If Impact had not led the way, we probably would have helped the wrong people in the wrong places and in the wrong way. We deeply appreciate Impact's leadership of the entire New Orleans effort."

In the end, 473 Black college students and young professionals gave up their spring breaks and vacations to be God's hands and feet of healing in the city. They found themselves forever changed as well. Howard University student Andrena Sawyer met Mr. Jones, a man stuck on his roof for three days and left homeless by the hurricane. Andrena led Mr. Jones to Christ and left him with $10 and her prayers.

Later that night at a gospel concert for the victims, Andrena saw Mr. Jones in the crowd and witnessed his new heart; he placed a bill into the collection box. "I'm pretty sure it was the $10 I gave him," she says. Upon leaving, Andrena said, "A part of me feels uneasy because I left work incomplete. A part of me is grateful for the amount of growth the Lord allowed me to experience. I feel liberated. Yet at the same time I feel silenced for the many people like Mr. Jones whose voice will never be heard."

The African-American churches were thrilled to see young Black students come to their rescue. Rebecca's pastor friends saw the return on years of generous giving, and their voices were heard.

Many of our alumni are serving in ways that we, as a movement, have difficulty documenting. I was in New York in the spring of 2008 and had dinner with Ryan and Charity (Shouse) Haygood. They had helped launch an Impact chapter at Colorado College as undergrads, and Ryan had been one of our first Impact fellows (interns) before going to law school. Charity told stories of her service as a vice principal at an inner-city middle school in Newark, New Jersey. They both shared their adventures as the youth directors at their church. Ryan asked me to pray for his upcoming case as an attorney for the NAACP Legal Defense and Education Fund. Ryan shared that he was arguing for the restoration of voting rights to convicted felons and explained how those laws were often put in place to remove Black people, men in particular, from the registered voter lists in the post-Reconstruction South. His motivation is that those who exit prison and want to become productive citizens would have the additional stake in their communities that voting provides. As Ryan shared, I stopped him and told him that he was living out the Impact vision in a most powerful way.

We also are committed to getting more African Americans overseas, particularly to be involved in missionary efforts in Africa and among the diaspora. This is important to the Black community for several reasons. The African-American community is still in the process of recovery from having had our cultures of origin stripped from us during slavery. Our appreciation for and understanding of our own culture will continue to be underdeveloped until we have made the pilgrimage to experience the motherland firsthand. I believe we have a stake in the future of the African continent. It is true that very few of us can trace our roots back to a specific people group. The reality is that the standard policy of slaveholders was to insure that people who spoke the same language were not on the same plantation or farm. Slave masters prohibited the speaking of African languages. What this means is that the families that emerged on these plantations were typically a union of Africans from different tribes. In the generations that followed, this mixing of tribes would have continued. Therefore, it is likely that most of us have the blood of a dozen African tribes coursing through our veins. In light of that, I claim kinship with all of sub-Saharan Africa!

Additionally, travel to Africa or other parts of the diaspora nations is the best way to drive home to African Americans the incredibly privileged position those of us in America enjoy. It is also apparent that those of us of African descent have a particular role to play in world evangelization. There are places we can go that our White brothers and sisters cannot. Our music, athletes, and entertainers are influencing the planet. As African Americans, do we really want the primary export of African-American culture to be the music and videos being produced by the hip hop and R & B industries? Not only are students willing to serve overseas, but we are seeing increasing numbers of our alumni participate in short-term missions. There is even more potential for us to send missionaries, both short and long-term, as we broaden our missions offerings to incorporate more compassion ministries. We want to bring the hope of the gospel to those who are distressed and in despair.

IGNITING A FIRE FOR GOD
BY MELODY COPENNY

Lecrae Moore had no intention of attending Impact '98 and didn't even know what The Impact Movement was really all about. As Christmas break approached, a Christian friend connected with the 19-year-old and told him about the event which would be taking place in Atlanta, GA. This sealed the deal for Lecrae. But he had no idea what God had in store for him and how his life would change for eternity.

Lecrae says that his experience at Impact '98 ignited a fire inside of him. "I saw all of these people hungry for the Word of God and excited," he says. "Keynote speaker, James White's message changed my life. It was at that point in time when I finally understood the gospel of Jesus Christ." Outside the doors of the conference he joined with other conferees during a day of outreach, hitting the streets of Atlanta and taking the message of God's love and forgiveness to whomever would hear. "I didn't know but 2 things—I once was blind and now I could see," he explains.

Impact '98 was a spiritual launching pad for Lecrae's new life as a believer. He returned to the University of North Texas, printed his testimony and passionately distributed it around campus. He also pursued fellowship, accountability and discipleship with other men who could mentor him in his growing faith. During the following years, Lecrae also uncovered a unique talent of his—music through rap and rhyme—a gift that God would soon use for His glory.

Today, Lecrae is a nationally-renowned Christian hip-hop artist and integral member of the cutting-edge Reach Records roster. He released his first album, *Real Talk* at the age of 24; an innovative sophomore project, *After the Music Stops*; and a widely successful third album, *Rebel*. Lecrae claimed the No. 3 position on iTunes' Rap chart in 2008 with this latest album.

Using his musical drive, gift for rhyme and heart for ministry, Lecrae's desire is to lead others to Christ, with a passion to see their lives forever changed like his was at Impact '98.

9
WHAT IS GOD UP TO?

GOD IS RAISING up a great movement of His Spirit in the hearts and minds of people of African descent. Our ancestors suffered, struggled, prayed, and cried, and God heard their prayers. It is now time for this generation of emerging Black leaders to take up the mantle and respond to the challenges that confront our community today. We must take action to address the reality that the public education system in our inner cities is failing nearly half our children. We have to restore the standard of biblical morality that is too often ignored, leaving our women to raise our children on their own and resulting in too many Black men in prison. We must teach the emerging generation of leaders to avoid the pitfalls of consumer debt and maximize the resources God will entrust to them for the sake of His kingdom. If we steward our resources well—not just our money, but also the expertise we have gained and the cultural heritage and spiritual legacy we have received—we can enter into the destiny to which God has called us.

The movement has begun. In 2007, we launched the first Impact music team after two summers of sending out summer music mission teams to use the power and persuasiveness of Black urban gospel and Christian hip-hop to gather crowds, gain a hearing, and clearly communicate the gospel. Based in Indianapolis as an expression of our partnership with Campus Crusade for Christ's Keynote Ministry, the teams have toured numerous cities in the U.S., have performed for thousands, and have seen hundreds indicate decisions for Christ. Moreover, this is just the beginning.

How can you help? We need you to pray, we need you to give, and we need you to join us.

We Ask You to Pray

Please don't take this call to pray lightly. I am dead earnest. We are taking on spiritual strongholds—some of which trace their roots back to Africa—that our enemy will not yield easily. We are engaging a struggle in the unseen realms, where the evil one has established the patterns and the power to make Whites and Blacks resent each other and compete with one another, even in the body of Christ. We need God to move, to empower our efforts, to go before us, and come behind us. As Jesus made clear in John 15:5, without Him we can do nothing.

We Invite You to Give

Whether you are Black, White, Brown, or "other," we implore you to get behind this emerging movement financially. Our long-term vision is to see the bulk of our funding come from communities of African descent. Some have interpreted that to mean that we do not want our White and other brothers and sisters to invest in this movement. Nothing could be further from the truth. It is true that I believe that a missionary endeavor is only healthy when its funding comes from the community it is serving. Yet, that does not mean that others should not have the opportunity of investing in that work and reaping the spiritual rewards of doing so. From time to time, someone questions why we, as a ministry, operate as a faith mission, funded by the giving of individuals and entities who want our mission to move forward. The answer is multi-faceted, but it can be boiled down to a very simple principle that is revealed in Philippians 4:17.

Philippians 4 is a much-loved, much-quoted passage of Scripture. The twenty-three verses of this chapter include several that are cherished and frequently referred to by Christians. You will quickly recognize them when you read them.

> Rejoice in the Lord always. I will say it again: Rejoice!
> —PHILIPPIANS 4:4

> Do not be anxious about anything, but in everything, by prayer and petition, with thanksgiving, present your requests to God. And the peace of God, which transcends all understanding, will guard your hearts and your minds in Christ Jesus.
> —PHILIPPIANS 4:6–7

> Finally, brothers, whatever is true, whatever is noble, whatever is right, whatever is pure, whatever is lovely, whatever is admirable—if anything is excellent or praiseworthy—think about such things.
> —PHILIPPIANS 4:8

> I can do everything through him who gives me strength.
> —PHILIPPIANS 4:13

> And my God will meet all your needs according to his glorious riches in Christ Jesus.
> —PHILIPPIANS 4:19

Now, aren't those familiar? However, there is another verse to which I want to draw your attention.

> Not that I am looking for a gift, but I am looking for what may be credited to your account.
> —PHILIPPIANS 4:17

In the context of a lengthy thank-you note, the apostle Paul describes his motivation, which is not to get money from the members of the church at Philippi but rather to allow them the privilege of making an investment that will yield eternal dividends for them. This principle, stated in summary here, is found in many other biblical passages, from Jesus' teaching in the Sermon on the Mount (Matt. 6:19–34) to Paul's instructions to his son in the ministry (1 Tim. 6:17–19). The overriding thought is this: those who give to the Lord's work are investing in eternal things and will be rewarded when they enter into that eternity. This has profound implications for those of us who are set apart as missionaries. A missionary is one who is sent to take the gospel to those who have never heard it or to those who are unable to provide support for the ministry they are receiving. This is in contrast to church-based ministries, which are funded by the congregation on which those ministries focus.

This principle makes it clear that while some respond with annoyance or resentment to our extension of the opportunity to give, we have no right to stop extending that opportunity to as many as we can. When we withhold that opportunity, we are being both selfish and poor stewards, and ultimately disobedient to clear Christian teaching.

Selfish?

Yes, selfish. We who are called to do the work of an evangelist as a vocation or even for a short season are granted a special privilege of cultivating and reaping spiritual fruit. That fruit— souls—is of eternal value to our heavenly Father, and the New Testament is clear that such service is rewarded in the life that is to come (2 John 8 and 3 John 8, 1 Cor. 3:5–15). If we seek to avoid giving people the opportunity to invest in us by supporting ourselves (sometimes called "tent-making") or seeking to create a business/ministry model that is self-funding, we are denying others who are not called as missionaries the opportunity to obtain a share or an interest in that which the Lord chooses to do through our service. Paul engaged in "tent-making," but the text suggests that he only did so out of necessity when his funding ran out. There are times in any missionary's life when such a choice may be necessary. But, if we remain in that mode beyond its necessity or seek to avoid asking others to give, it is as if we are hoarding our spiritual rewards to be enjoyed by us alone when we get to heaven. Is that not a selfish way to behave? Is it not better, more selfless, to give others the opportunity to "buy in" by giving support to our ministry?

A Question of Stewardship

In the case of The Impact Movement, the stewardship implications are quite obvious. God has blessed this ministry with incredible fruitfulness. This work is growing organically. Those who have been touched by this ministry are reaching out to others and telling their friends from campus to campus, city to city. Believers are seeking us out, asking variations of the question, How can I start an Impact chapter on my campus or in my city or town?

The sad reality is that the growth of this movement is limited by our ability to respond in a timely manner to the requests that come our way. We get e-mails and phone calls daily; our struggle is to keep up with the inquiries. The reason we struggle is that our people are out working on their personal funding or we are unable to hire personnel to handle some of the administrative and technical assistance we need to free our missionary staff and fellows to engage the ever-growing interest in this movement. We must invite others to invest in this work, participating through their giving, so that those of us who are participating through their service are free to do just that—serve. So, it is a matter of stewardship for those of us who are full-time leaders with Impact (Luke 12:48). Also, it is a matter of stewardship for those who have the means to aid us (3 John 5–8). It boils down to obedience.

First Corinthians 9:1–14 describes the right of a missionary/ minister to derive his/her living from the preaching of the gospel. The apostle Paul goes on in verse 18 of 1 Corinthians 9 to describe his practice of offering the gospel "free of charge." Jesus, when he sent out the Seventy-two, instructed them not to take a cloak or a bag but to look for people to support their ministry by housing and feeding them (Luke 10). Jesus Himself was supported by Mary, Susanna, Joanna, and other women (Luke 8:1–3). All of these examples speak of the propriety of allowing others to support those who are working in the ministry. It only makes sense that if we are to follow Jesus' example and that of the apostle Paul, we must be open to giving people the opportunity to invest in our ministry. To do otherwise would be disobedient.

We are instructed by Jesus to preach the gospel. What we typically think of when we think of preaching may be misleading. We think a preacher operates from a pulpit and may conclude that other forms of communication are excluded. The original word that is translated "preach" in the New Testament is the same word translated "herald." In ancient times, heralds were sent from one king or leader to another kingdom or its people. They would proclaim their message in the court of the king or in the public square so that the maximum number of people had the opportunity to hear it. By using that word, Jesus calls us to get out of the traditional places of worship and Christian assembly to get the word out in the public arena. In the time of His earthly ministry, that was at the market, on the seashore, on the side of a mountain, and in private homes, as well as in the temple and synagogues. In our day, the public arena involves the Internet, television, radio, DVDs, podcasts, and an array of other media. We humbly yet unapologetically invite you to invest in this ministry, to help us get the message out using all of these media. Your investment will bear "interest" into all eternity. These uncertain times have underscored the fact that there is no better investment that one can make.

So, please invite others, Black or not, to invest as well. You can do so by going online to www.impactmovement.com.

WE WANT YOU TO JOIN US

No matter what your ethnicity, we invite you to come serve with The Impact Movement for a season or for a lifetime. Jesus said it well when He declared that, "The harvest is plentiful but the workers are few" (Matt. 9:37). In the case of The Impact Movement, we need a number of positions to be filled, from campus coaches and community engagement specialists to accountants, writers, graphic designers, information technologists, marketing experts, fundraisers, and event planners. That is just a sampling of the opportunities for service. Or, you can volunteer your time. We are developing a number of task forces of volunteers with a variety of areas of expertise who are giving some of their time to help move us forward in critical areas. You can find out more about these opportunities on our Web site or by calling 888-672-2896 for more information.

REFLECTIONS ON PSALM 102

One of the things I love about our spiritual heritage as Black people is the way in which our forefathers found in the Bible their hope, help, and perspective on life. It has been my goal, my objective, my habit to honor that heritage, not just as historical awareness, not just as a cultural peculiarity, but as a living practice. I believe based on experience and on the witness of Scripture that this is exactly what God desires from us. The Bible is not just a bedtime storybook, nor a book of inspirational fables. It is the Word of God. It is true, has come true, is coming true, and will continue to come true until this thing we call time is no more.

Several years ago, when I was approaching the end of our time in ministry at Howard University, I reached a crisis of hope; not of belief, not of faith, but of hope. You see, I believed (and still do) that God is and that He is a rewarder of those who diligently seek Him (Heb. 11:6). I had faith that He is the same God today as He was in the days of Moses, Elijah, and Jesus (Heb. 13:8). My problem was that I was losing hope that He would bring about the changes in my day that would allow me to fulfill the call He placed on my life. He called me to invest myself in a movement that would sweep the African-American community with the truth and power of the gospel; a movement that would cause us, as a people, to capitalize on the tremendous opportunity we have been given because we live in this country and have access to its resources; a movement that would lead us to become a reflection of His redemptive power and proclaim that power to a lost and dying world. I was losing hope that this would happen.

In the course of my daily devotions, the Lord brought me to Psalm 102. In this psalm the writer describes his anguish over the fate that has befallen him and Jerusalem. There is no author indicated in the text, yet the context suggests that it is a psalm written during the Babylonian captivity. It is written from the vantage point of an individual, yet it addresses the plight of the nation, particularly in its reference to Zion, the name for the capital city of Judah, Jerusalem. Perhaps its writer was one of the Davidic kings in exile, or maybe it was written by Daniel, whose prayer in Daniel 9 seems to mirror this refrain.

This psalm initially describes the sorrow and suffering its writer was experiencing. Yet, when he turns his attention toward God, he sees something else. There are three things the psalmist speaks of that give him hope. He reflects on God's character, God's acts, and God's purposes. He speaks of God's character being timeless (v. 12), unchanging (vv. 24-27), and worthy of fear and glory (vv. 15-16). He rehearses many of God's acts, such as His discipline (vv. 10, 23), His intervention (v. 13), His acts of restoration (v. 16), His response to prayer (v. 17), and His deliverance (vv. 19-20). He summarizes all of this with a major revelation of God's purpose in verses 18-22. The writer declares that God's intention is for the story of God's dealing with Israel to be recorded so that future generations—representatives of people groups not yet in existence at the time of that recording—would read, hear, and realize that God is a God of justice, mercy, deliverance, and restoration. That God takes a special interest in those who cry out to Him in their suffering, those who are facing condemnation. This passage makes clear that God's purpose is to use His Word to inspire, motivate, captivate, and ultimately regenerate a people in order that they might praise Him in the great eschatological dawn (vv. 21-22).

This is the story of my people, Africans in America, and of others of the African diaspora. We have no exclusive claim on this experience. God's intention is that people groups from around the globe would experience His transforming power in order to create that multi-ethnic, multi-lingual chorus that will revisit the foreshadowing of heaven at the Day of Pentecost (Acts 2). That day in Jerusalem, the believers were together and started speaking in languages they had not learned, and those looking on heard the gospel being proclaimed and God praised in their own languages. Revelation 7:9 indicates that this intelligible clamor of praise will happen again around the throne and that it will continue into eternity.

Moreover, the promise implied in Psalm 102:18-22 is that when a people groan, when they cry out to God, He will remember, He will visit, He will act on their behalf. God has acted on behalf of Black people in this country. God did hear the groaning of our ancestors. An appointed time has come, in which God remembered our people's suffering and has blessed us with great prosperity. He has done His part. Therefore, it is time for us to do ours.

It is time for us to stop living for ourselves. Time for us to start acting like the children of God we are. Time for us to take our rightful place in His service. Time for us to stop defining our worth by what White folk are doing, saying, or thinking. Time for us to stop selling our bodies, our talents, or our brains for "a crust of bread or such."

It is time for us to recognize the incredible blessing it is to be an African-American Christian—spiritually, economically, educationally, culturally—and to get about the work of speaking to our culture. We are drifting away from God. I am not just alluding to the "left behinds," the thugs, gang-bangers, drug runners, and drug users, the "babies" who are making babies. I am also addressing those who want to run away from our community, the affluent, high-achieving, social climbing, self-indulgent, designer-clothing-wearing, credit card-wielding posers and pretenders.

It is time that we stop living in debt, time that we denounce the slave master morality and set out to live up to biblical standards, time that we stopped putting our personal career, prestige, and materialistic goals ahead of God's priorities and purposes. Our obligation is to invest all we have for maximum spiritual increase. That is what The Impact Movement is all about.

Our ancestors found comfort in the record of God's dealing with the children of Israel. In that account they were taught or reminded that God is a good God, that He is a plan-working God, that He is just as well as merciful, and that He will one day make all things right, punishing the wicked and rewarding the faithful. With that faith our ancestors endured, praying and crying, preaching and teaching, sinning and being forgiven. They laid a foundation for us today. We owe it to them to honor their sacrifices on our behalf by building on that foundation to honor God, lift up those who are falling down among us, and proclaim to the world the manifold grace, mercy, and redemptive power of God.

My father died in March 2006. He had pastored the First Baptist Church of Vandalia, which sits on a hill overlooking Charleston in the Kanawha River valley of West Virginia, for over forty years. A civil rights activist and community developer, he had known senators, governors, and served on numerous boards. In the summer of 2005, he had one of the final crises of his long battle with cardiovascular disease, and all of his children were called back to West Virginia. I took a turn sitting with him through the night in the hospital, helping him to the restroom when he needed assistance, and generally making sure he was as comfortable as he could be. That night in the late watches, he started asking me about our work with The Impact Movement. In the dim light of a darkened hospital room, he said, "That's a great work you and Becky are doing. Don't stop. Stay on the wall." In those few words, he was referring to one of the classic sermons of the Black preaching tradition: "Watchman, Stay on the Wall." That sermon, based on Ezekiel 3 and 33, speaks of the prophet's responsibility to warn the people of impending danger and to tell those people of the opportunity for repentance. It takes that principle from that Old Testament passage and applies it to modern-day preachers.

My father blessed me that night. In that brief phrase, he reminded me of the rich spiritual tradition in which I stand. He affirmed the value and significance of the undertaking to which God has called me. He admonished me not to give up and to remember that if I failed to fulfill my responsibility, I would have to answer to my Lord. My father left me with a commendation and a confirmation of the calling I had been given. That calling is to challenge my people, Black people, to love and serve God and to make the most of these earthly opportunities, because they are a gift, a privilege, a stewardship that we must not fail to exercise well. Failure to do so will result in great pain and suffering and an increase in calamity and frustration. If we choose wisely, God will grant us the privilege of being a reflection of His redemptive power, bringing glory and honor to Him here in this country, on the continent of Africa, and around the world. May God grant us that grace. May we fulfill that destiny and help prepare the way for our Lord's return.

> Let this be written for a future generation, that a people not yet created may praise the LORD: "The LORD looked down from his sanctuary on high, from heaven he viewed the earth, to hear the groans of the prisoners and release those condemned to death." So the name of the LORD will be declared in Zion and his praise in Jerusalem when the peoples and the kingdoms assemble to worship the LORD.
>
> —PSALM 102:18–22

EPILOGUE

J
ust off Route 25 in Malden, West Virginia, an old clapboard church sits on the old highway, now a side road, with its back to the railroad tracks. Booker T. Washington taught Sunday school here before he walked and hitchhiked four hundred miles to attend Hampton Institute in 1872. The African Zion Baptist Church, built in 1857, is the oldest Black Baptist church in West Virginia, now listed on the National Register of Historic Places.

My father served as the church's pastor and caretaker in the years of my childhood. On Saturdays once a month, he used to pile a lawnmower, a vacuum cleaner, tools, and his five children into the back of the family station wagon. We would drive twenty miles to that little old church to get it ready for the afternoon services scheduled for the next day. I ran the vacuum cleaner on the red carpet strip up the center aisle. I wiped down the roughly constructed, brown-painted pews. I mowed the dusty, small square of grass in the front, sometimes "catching" poison ivy when I would trim the straggly hedge.

I didn't realize it then, but those Saturdays were a window into my spiritual heritage. My mother's great-grandpa Brown was one of the builders of that church. He was a praying man. They say that he would weep as he prayed and that his petitions were offered with such intensity that he would inch around the church on his knees, wringing his hands and pleading with God for the deliverance of our people. Sometimes he prayed so hard that he couldn't walk on his knees anymore and would simply huddle over a pew. Another ancestor, my great-great-great-grandfather, a slave who escaped to Canada, died eleven days after preaching his last sermon as an AME minister in 1877. Both of these men knew oppression, for they both had been slaves and lived under Jim Crow segregation. They also knew heartache; Grandpa Brown's daughter had a child out of wedlock, fathered by an unnamed White man. That child was my grandmother.

So, godliness is not my only heritage. As I reflect on the generations that have followed, my extended family has had its share of addiction, infidelity, and child abuse. While my family has reared educators, doctors, political leaders, war heroes, and business executives, some of us have also been the object of paternity suits, spent time in jail, and suffered injuries in gang violence. I guess you could say we are an average African-American family. We are blessed with a rich legacy of those who went before, sought to serve God, and pleaded with Him on behalf of their families and our people. But we also have a legacy of those who made and continue to make poor choices, creating yet another illustration for those who would denigrate our people.

Every time I think about those Saturdays I spent as a child cleaning that little church in Malden, West Virginia, I get goose bumps, and I get a little misty. I realize that what I am doing now must be, at least partially, a result of the prayers of my great-great-great-grandfather Richard Thomas and my great-great-grandpa Brown. I doubt that they knew that one of their descendants would graduate from an Ivy League school. Yet, through it all, they left us the testimony that they cried out to God. I have an extraordinarily rich heritage. My family is not without its flaws and tragic failures, but I have known for a long time that I have been given something on which I am to build. Paul wrote to Timothy in 2 Timothy 1:5–6 that, in light of his family heritage and the heritage he had received from Paul himself, Timothy had an imperative to continue that building process. As a child, I did not know what this meant. Now that I am a man, I know.

"Lest our hearts, drunk with the wine of the world, we forget Thee..." James Weldon Johnson penned these words over a hundred years ago in the third stanza of "Lift Every Voice and Sing," the song that became known as the Negro national anthem. My parents taught me that during segregation this song was sung regularly in Black schools. It is still played before every home football game at Howard University. Sadly, his prayer, sounding words of warning, seems prophetic now. We have achieved much. Our people are entering the middle class in unprecedented numbers. The educational achievement of African Americans is greater than it has ever been. African-American athletes and entertainers are marketed all over the world. Our people head some of the largest corporations in the world, such as Time-Warner (Richard Parsons) and American Express (Ken Chenault). The Kerner Commission report of 1968 stated, "Our nation is moving toward two societies, one black, one white—separate and unequal."[1] Census Bureau data for that year reveals that Blacks where roughly three and one-half times as likely to live below the poverty level as White Americans.[2] By 2006, the gap had closed. Twenty four and three tenths percent of Black people lived in poverty, which was nearly two and two-fifths times higher than Whites.[3] That is progress, but no one would say that this amount of change is enough. Moreover, the prospects for decreasing that number are daunting.

As we have begun to explore in this work, these problems have solutions. Those solutions are rooted in our biblical faith, which has so often given strength to those who went before us. Christian faith is the foundation on which we can build a clear outlook. We can't allow our mistakes or the mistakes of those we love, respect, or admire to keep us from affirming and pursuing what is true. Nor can we allow our as-yet-unsuccessful efforts to cause us to give up the struggle.

The Impact Movement is struggling to secure the funding necessary to maintain, much less expand, its reach. I am not sure what the future holds. But, as the song says, "I know who holds the future." The Black community is uniquely positioned in the world to glorify our Creator. We are uniquely positioned in history to help usher in the end of the age. It will come. Our choices will shape where we fit in the drama that unfolds on "That Great Gettin'-up Mornin'." Our ancestors look forward to that day. May this generation and the ones that follow live in such a way that we can all look forward to that day as well.

To Contact the Author

Cryofhope@impactmovement.com

THE IMPACT MOVEMENT COMMITMENT

W E OF THE Impact Movement are committed to the lordship of Jesus Christ being manifest in the experience of those of African descent. We are persuaded of the uniqueness of Jesus in history and the efficacy and necessity of His sacrifice on the cross to provide salvation. We respond to Jesus when He says, "I am the way, the truth and the life. No one comes to the Father except through Me" (John 14:6).

We commit ourselves to the development of an expression of the incarnation of Christ within cultures of African descent (1 Cor. 9:22). We believe that these cultures are destined to be reflections of the redemptive power of God's Son, Jesus Christ. We are committed to the Great Commission (Matt. 28:16–20) and will use every means at our disposal to bring the greatest glory to our heavenly Father, winning the maximum number of souls to the Savior; discipling those who respond to our witness; and mobilizing as many as possible to take the truth of Jesus Christ to the campus, the community, and the world.

Therefore, in reliance on God's Holy Spirit and by His power, I do declare my commitment to:

God's Word

I will study the Scriptures to show myself approved to God as a workman who needs not be ashamed (2 Tim. 2:15). I will not allow my technical or professional expertise to outstrip my biblical fluency. I realize my need for a critically developed, biblically based, Christ-centered worldview by which I evaluate all of life.

A Bold Witness

I will tell all with whom I am given opportunity about the matchless grace of God as displayed through His Son, Jesus Christ (2 Tim. 4:2). He is the only hope for our peoples (Prov. 14:34) and for all of mankind (Acts 4:12).

True Worship

My devotion to God will be characterized by authenticity, integrity, and consistency (John 4:24). I will lift my hands and voice in adoration and praise of my Maker, Redeemer, and Friend. He is the Source of my joy, strength, peace, power, and purpose. To Him and Him alone do I bend my knee (Ps. 95).

Godly Living

I will seek to live in a manner worthy of my calling (Eph. 4:1). Faith without works is dead (James 2:14). I will manifest my faith in my living. This includes a commitment to biblical standards of morality (1 Thess. 4:3) and financial responsibility (Rom. 13:8), no matter how much or how little He entrusts to me.

Redemptive Work

I am called to good works, which God prepared for me beforehand (Eph. 2:10). I will do good to all, especially to those of the household of faith (Gal. 6:10). I will seek to undo the work of the evil one, heal those harmed by the sin of mankind and ameliorate the sufferings inherent in a fallen world.

Global Vision

I will do everything in my power to see this message declared to the maximum number of people (Phil. 3:7). This will require the investment of my time, my talents, and my treasure in the reproduction of godly leadership (2 Tim. 2:2). I have a responsibility to see the gospel spread around the world.

And so I do offer my life in obedience to my King, and to the service of His kingdom. I will pray, fast, study, give, preach, and teach to impact the emerging generation of those of African descent with the reality, relevance, and essential nature of a relationship with God through Jesus Christ. May He use us to draw hundreds of thousands of people to a saving knowledge of Him, beginning with those in my vicinity, extending to those of African descent generally, encompassing those of various ethnicities in my country, and ultimately reaching around the world, with a special concern for Africa and the African diaspora (Acts 1:8; Ps. 68:31).

To Jesus be all the glory!

SIGNATURE_____

DATE

NOTES

Chapter 3
EXPLORATIONS OF RECONCILIATION

1.   "White Privilege: Unpacking the Invisible Knapsack," excerpted from working paper 189, "White Privilege and Male Privilege: A Personal Account of Coming to See Correspondences Through Work in Women's Studies" (1988), by Peggy McIntosh, Wellesley College Center for Research on Women, Wellesley, MA.

Chapter 6
THE EMERGENCE OF A MOVEMENT

1.   Dr. Bright was a great encourager of ours as well. He did not always understand why we were doing things the way that we were, but his bottom line was always whether or not more people were hearing about Jesus. Just days before his passing to be with the Lord, he personally wrote a support check with an encouraging note to Rebecca and me.

2.   The name InterCultural Resources was changed in the late 1990s to "Ethnic Student Ministries" in order to reflect our emphasis on reaching ethnic students, not just equipping white staff to reach ethnic students.

Chapter 7
WHY IS THIS NECESSARY?

1.   Ralph Winter, "A New Day in Ministry to Native Americans," *Mission Frontiers* (September 2000).

2.   A. Ragoonan, N. Shrestha, and W. Smith, "Advertising in Black Magazines: Do Advertisements Reflect African American Consumer Behavior?" *Services Marketing Quarterly* 27 (2, 2005): 67.

3.　　p. 479, King, Martin Luther, Jr., *A Testament of Hope: the Essential Writings and Speeches of Martin Luther King, Jr.*, edited by James Melvin Washington. HarperCollins, New York, New York. 1986. This quote is from Dr. King's 1958 book, *Stride Toward Freedom: The Montgomery Story.*

4.　　"Existing Stereotypes about African-Americans Are Way Off the Mark and Impede Reconciliation," The Barna Group, http://www.barna.org/FlexPage.aspx?Page=BarnaUpdate&BarnaUpdateID =42 (accessed February 6, 2009).

5.　　Timothy C. Morgan, "Racist No More? Black Leaders Ask," *Christianity Today* (8/01/1995), www.ChristianityToday.com.

Chapter 8
The Impact Movement, Inc.

1.　　Ragoonan, Shrestha, and Smith: 65–88.

2.　　John S. Mbiti, *African Religions and Philosophy* (London: Heinemann, 1969), 229, as cited in John P. Kealy and David W. Shenk, *The Early Church and Africa* (Nairobi: Oxford University Press, 1975), 1.

3.　　"Break Out the Champagne: Let's Celebrate Some Important News on the Progress…" *The Journal of Blacks in Higher Education* 52 (Summer 2006), Ethnic NewsWatch (ENW): 38.

Epilogue

1.　　*Report of the National Advisory Commission on Civil Disorders* (New York: Bantam Books, 1968), 1.

2.　　"Poverty Status of Persons, by Family Relationship, Race, and Hispanic Origin: 1959 to 1993," U.S. *Bureau of the Census, CD-ROM Income and Poverty*, 1993. In 1968, 10 percent of Whites lived below the poverty line; 24.3 percent of Blacks lived below that line.

3.　　"Table 2. Poverty Status of People by Family Relationship, Race, and Hispanic Origin: 1959 to 2007," U.S. Bureau of the Census, Current Population Survey, Annual Social and Economic Supplements.

PRODUCT OFFERINGS FROM THE IMPACT MOVEMENT

The Passage

In pre-Civil War America, thousands of African Americans escaped to freedom by way of the Underground Railroad, a secret network of relationships and safe houses. Harriet Tubman, an escaped slave herself, returned to conduct others to freedom nineteen different times via this passage.

Many of us today, while physically free, still experience various forms of bondage. There is still a need for spiritual and lasting freedom

This booklet will help you consider four principles that describe the passage to true freedom and a personal relationship with God.

Price: $4.95 for a package of 25

The Journey

Check out *The Journey,* the latest Bible study resource from The Impact Movement! This six-week resource is packaged in a journal format and covers the foundations of the Christian faith. This study can be done individually or in a group setting. Students receive a special student rate of $5.00. In addition, students can save money by purchasing *The Journey* through our special group cost.

Price: $10.00

The Grill (CD-ROM)

The Grill is Impact's latest evangelism tool and resource designed to meet the needs of our African-American emerging leaders in a relevant context. Whether for the individual or for a group, use *The Grill* to access Bible studies, music, and video clips wherever you are!

Price: $14.99

Inspired (CD)

Join Infinit Impact, the music group of The Impact Movement, in boldly proclaiming your purpose and position in Jesus Christ through *Inspired* These soul-stirring songs, *inspired* by conferences hosted by The Impact Movement, are the soundtrack for a generation *inspired* to pursue a passion for God. This is your chance to hear that passion wherever you go. Get *inspired*!

Price: $5.00

**AVAILABLE NOW AT
WWW.IMPACTMOVEMENT.COM**

(YOU MAY ALSO ORDER AT 1-888-672-2896.)

MEET JESUS: A GOSPEL PRESENTATION FROM *THE PASSAGE*
Check Out the Truth!

WHAT IS TRUTH? Who has it? Let's face it—in today's world, it's hard to know what's true anymore. How's your journey going? Has your search for real answers only led you down a dead end? Truth is more than just talk. Real truth is soul bending. It's deep, profound, and life changing. We invite you to find this truth via *The Passage*.

1. GOD'S DESIRE

God created you in His image. He wants you to know Him personally, so you may experience the love, peace, and freedom He offers.

God's design

So God created man in his own image, in the image of God He created him; male and female He created them.

—GENESIS 1:27

God's love

For God so loved the world, that He gave his one and only Son, that whoever believes in him shall not perish but have eternal life.

—JOHN 3:16

God's plan

> Now this is eternal life: that they may know you, the
> only true God, and Jesus Christ, whom you have sent.
>
> —JOHN 17:3

What prevents us from experiencing the life of love and the
destiny God desires for us?

2. OUR REFUSAL

*Sin keeps us from knowing God personally and
from experiencing His love, peace, and freedom. Sin
enslaves, blocks, and separates us from God.*

People are sinful

> For all have sinned and fall short of the glory of God.
>
> —ROMANS 3:23

Sin is our innate refusal to go God's way and instead, to go
our own way and do our own thing. God is holy, that is, perfect
in who He is and all He does. Our sinful nature and actions
offend God's nature and result in a broken relationship and
separation from Him.

People are enslaved

> Jesus replied, "I tell you the truth, everyone who sins is
> a slave to sin."
>
> —JOHN 8:34

People are separated

> For the wages of sin is death [spiritual separation from
> God and His life].
>
> —ROMANS 6:23

Wages = Penalty

People are sinful and separated from a holy God by a great gap. We may try to cross that gap by living a good life, not harming anyone, attending church or other religious meetings, or by giving money to our favorite charities. All of these efforts fail because the sinful condition of the heart remains unchanged, enslaved to sin.

3. THE PASSAGE

The third principle below explains the only way to cross the gap.

Jesus Christ came to provide the passage back to God. Jesus Christ alone forgives and removes our sins so we can know God personally, and experience His love, peace, and freedom forever.

He died on the cross in our place

For Christ died for sins once for all, the righteous for the unrighteous, to bring you to God.

—1 PETER 3:18

Jesus Christ was able to pay the penalty for our sins because He is free from sin. Even His enemies could not find Him guilty of any wrongdoing.

He rose from the dead

Christ died for our sins…He was buried, He was raised on the third day according to the Scriptures…He appeared to Peter, and then to the Twelve. After that, He appeared to more than five hundred of the brothers.

—1 CORINTHIANS 15:3–6

Christ's resurrection proved that He has the power over death to enable us to live eternally with God.

He is the way to God

> Jesus answered, "I am the way and the truth and the life. No one comes to the Father except through me."
> —JOHN 14:6

He sets us free

> So if the Son sets you free, you will be free indeed.
> —JOHN 8:36

He sent His Son, Jesus Christ, to die on the cross for our sins, in our place. In this way He paid the death penalty that we deserve.

What would a person need to do in order to change their destiny to know God and experience the love and freedom from sin that He offers?

4. OUR RESPONSE

We must individually receive Jesus Christ, because only He provides the passage to God. Only then can we experience His love and live in freedom for eternity.

We must receive Christ

> Yet to all who received Him, to those who believed in His name, He gave the right to become children of God.
> —JOHN 1:12

We receive Christ through faith

> By grace you have been saved through faith; and that not of yourselves, it is the gift of God; not as a result of works that no one should boast.
> —EPHESIANS 2:8–9, NASB

Faith = trust, dependence on God

When we receive Christ, we experience His love, freedom, and eternal life.

> [Jesus speaking] I came that they might have life, and might have it abundantly.
> —JOHN 10:10, NASB

We receive Jesus Christ by faith, as an act of our will.

To receive Christ:

1. Recognize and admit you need to be forgiven of your sins.

2. Admit you can do nothing on your own to free yourself from your sins.

3. Turn away from your sins (repentance) and place your trust in Jesus Christ alone.

4. When you trust Christ, you receive His complete forgiveness and an eternal relationship with God.

Knowing intellectually that Jesus Christ is the Son of God is not enough. Having an emotional experience will not change your destiny and allow you to experience His love, peace, and freedom. *We receive Jesus Christ by faith, as an act of our will.*

5. Think About It

There are two kinds of lives or paths that people choose...

Self-directed life

Christ is outside the life. The different areas of life are self-directed and not in harmony with God's desires.

Christ-directed life

Christ is in the life. This person has received Christ and His forgiveness for their sins. Christ directs every area of life, resulting in harmony with God's desire and plan.

Which one represents your life right now?

Which one would you like to represent your life?

You can receive Christ right now by faith through prayer. (Prayer is just talking with God.) God is not so concerned with your words as He is with the attitude of your heart. You must mean what you pray, for God knows your heart and you cannot deceive Him. Here is a suggested prayer:

Jesus Christ, I need You. I confess that I have sinned against You and have been running my own life. Thank You for dying on the cross for my sins. Please come into my life and forgive my sins and set me free. Begin directing my life. Change my destiny. Make me into the person You created me to be. Thank you for answering my prayer by coming into my life and giving me eternal life. Amen.

Does this prayer express your heart's desire? If it does, pray this prayer right now and Christ will come into your life, as He promised.

6. How to Know...

How to know that Christ is in your life

Did you ask Christ to come into your life? How do you know He answered your prayer and came into your life? You can know that Christ is in your life because of 1 John 4:14–15:

> And we have seen and testify that the Father has sent His Son to be the Savior of the world. If anyone acknowledges that Jesus is the Son of God, God lives in him, and he in God.

God and His Word are completely trustworthy.

The Bible promises eternal life to all who receive Christ

> And the witness is this, that God has given us eternal life, and this life is in His Son. He who has the Son has life; he who does not have the Son of God does not have life. These things I have written to you who believe in the name of the Son of God, in order that you may know that you have eternal life.
> —1 John 5:11–13, nasb

Thank God daily that Christ is in your life and He will never leave you (Hebrews 13:5). You can know on the basis of His promise that Christ lives in you and you have eternal life, from the moment you invited Him in. He will not deceive you.

What if you don't feel any different?

Do not depend on feelings

This train diagram illustrates the relationship between fact (God and His Word), faith (our trust in God and His Word), and feeling (the result of our faith and obedience). Read John 14:21.

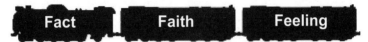

| Fact | Faith | Feeling |

The train will run with or without the caboose (feeling). In the same way, we as Christians do not depend on feelings or emotions. We rely on the promises of God's Word, not our feelings. The Christian lives by faith in God and His Word.

7. Enjoying God

The moment you received Christ by faith, as an act of your will, many things happened, including the following:

1. Christ came into your life (1 Corinthians 6:17; Colossians 1:27).

2. Christ set you free from your sins and forgave you (Romans 8:1–2; 2 Corinthians 3:17; Galatians 5:1; Colossians 1:14).

3. You became a child of God (John 1:12).

4. God lavished His love on you (Romans 8:35–39; 1 John 3:1).

5. You received eternal life (John 5:24).

6. You began the new and satisfying life for which God created you (John 10:10; 2 Corinthians 5:17; 1 Thessalonians 5:18).

Being freed and loved by Christ is the most important thing

that can happen to you! Would you like to thank God in prayer right now for what He has done for you? By thanking God, you demonstrate your faith.

To enjoy your new relationship with God to the fullest…

Suggestions for Christian growth

Our relationship with Christ grows as we trust God more and more with every detail of our lives. "The righteous will live by faith" (Galatians 3:11). This trust develops as we:

- **G**o to God in prayer daily (Colossians 4:2).

- **R**ead God's Word daily (Acts 17:11). Begin with the Gospel of John.

- **O**bey God moment by moment (John 14:21).

- **W**itness for Christ by your life and words (Matthew 4:19; John 15:8).

Get involved in a good church

God's Word admonishes us not to forsake "the assembling of ourselves together" (Hebrews 10:25; Acts 2:42–47). Several logs burn brightly together, but put one aside and its fire goes out. So it is with your relationship to other Christians. If you do not belong to a church, do not wait to be invited. Take the first step; call the pastor of a nearby church where Christ is honored and His Word is preached. Start this week and make plans to attend regularly.

If you've made a decision for Christ, we'd love to know! Contact The Impact Movement at info@impactmovement.com. For those who have already trusted Christ, we encourage you to share this truth with your friends, family, and others.